PICTURE IT

maps, graphs, charts, time lines, photographs

LES RICHARDS / MARGARET LEIER

PICTURE IT

maps, graphs, charts, time lines, photographs

Globe/Modern Curriculum Press

Toronto

Canadian Cataloguing in Publication Data

Richards, Leslie
    Picture it : maps, graphs, charts, time lines, photographs

Includes index.
ISBN 0-88996-152-2

1. Maps – Juvenile literature. 2. Photographic
interpretation – Juvenile literature.
3. Geography – Graphic methods – Juvenile
literature. I. Leier, Margaret. II. Title.

GA130.R53 1989   912   C88-094674-1

EDITOR: Sharon Ord Delisle
DESIGNER: John Zehethofer
ILLUSTRATORS: Acorn Illustration & Art Studio
                Ralph Oesterreich
                Nancy Cook
COVER PHOTO: Birgitte Nielsen
TYPESETTING: Jay Tee Graphics Ltd.

Printed and bound in Canada by The Bryant Press Limited

0 9 8 7 6 5 4 3 2

Contents

A Picture of You

Each one of us is a special person. In many ways we are all alike, but in many ways we are all different.

Look at a photograph of yourself.

- Are you tall, medium, or short?
- What colour are your eyes?
- What colour is your skin?

- What colour is your hair?
- Is your hair long or short?
- Is your hair straight or curly?

Draw a picture of you.

S. Ord

Heslop

A Look at the Classroom

Here are three ways of looking at the same classroom. Can you tell how objects in the classroom seem to change when they are looked at in different ways? How are these pictures the same? How are they different?

View from
a student's desk.

View from a ladder.

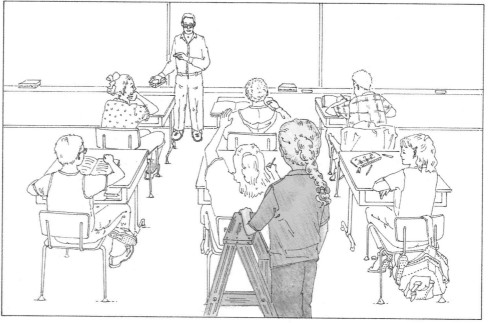

View as a fly on the ceiling would see the classroom.

The fly's viewpoint on the ceiling is the same viewpoint a mapmaker uses in drawing a map.

Draw your classroom as you think a fly on the ceiling would see it.

Around the Neighbourhood

This is a map of a neighbourhood.

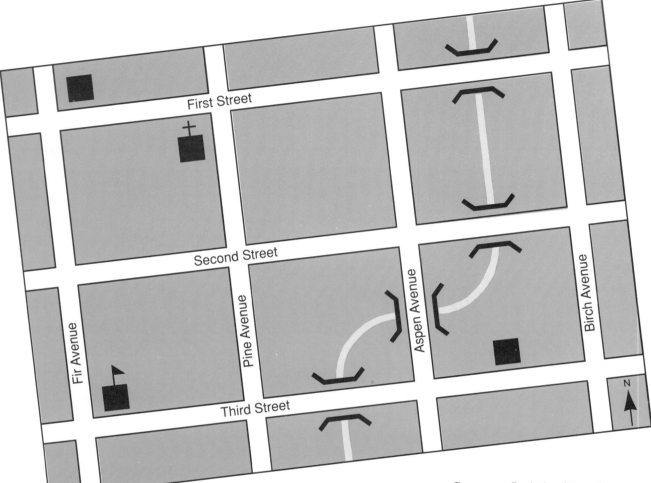

Can you find the blue line on the map? What does this blue line show? What do you think the symbol)(means?

Can you see the arrow in the lower right-hand corner of the map? What does this arrow show?

Describe how you would go from the house on Third Street to the church on Pine Avenue.

Where Are You?

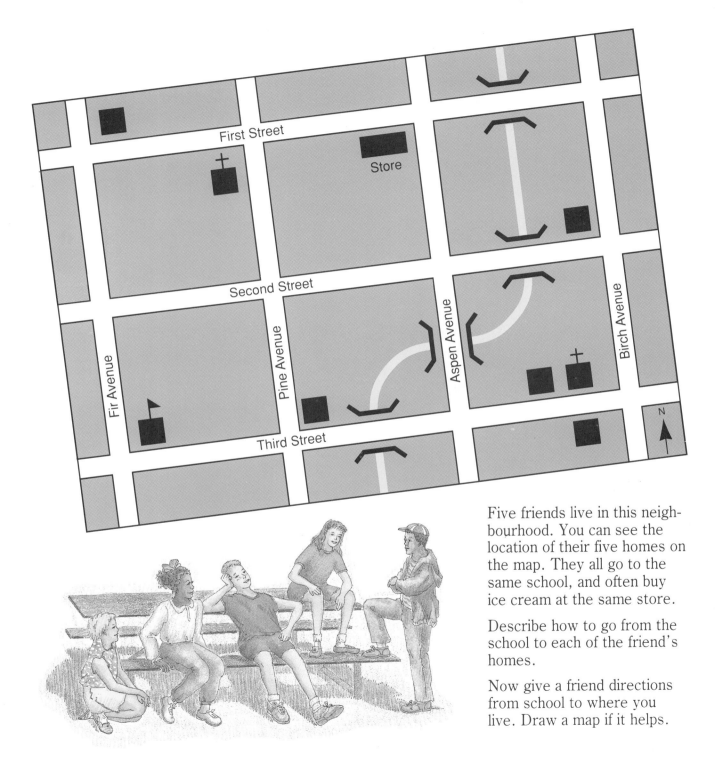

Five friends live in this neighbourhood. You can see the location of their five homes on the map. They all go to the same school, and often buy ice cream at the same store.

Describe how to go from the school to each of the friend's homes.

Now give a friend directions from school to where you live. Draw a map if it helps.

Symbols Stand for Real Things

On the last two pages you can see how drawings are used to stand for real objects. These drawings are called *symbols*. Every map has symbols on it that stand for real objects.

The symbols are listed in one part of the map with their meanings. The part of a map that lists the symbols is called a *legend*.

The following two pages show some symbols that are often used on maps. You will need to know these symbols to understand the maps which follow, and also so you can make your own maps.

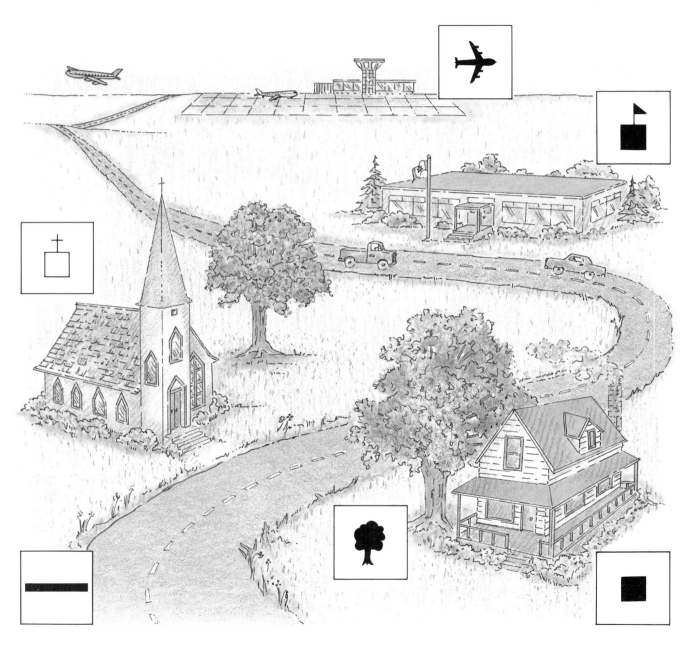

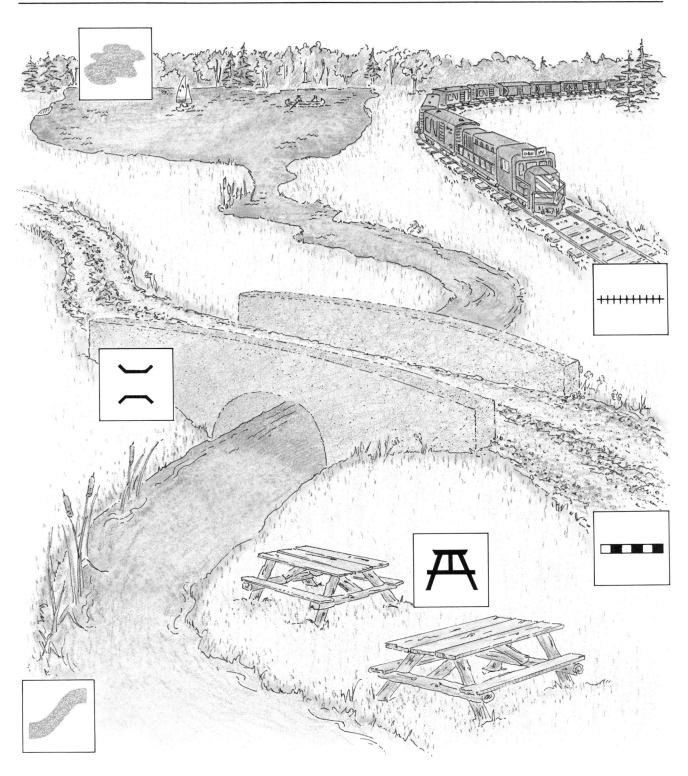

What Do You See?

Imagine it is a pleasant day and you decide to go for a long walk to a friend's house. You leave your house by the river bridge and follow the route shown on the map by a broken line.

Describe what you see on the walk. To do this you will need to know what the symbols in the legend mean.

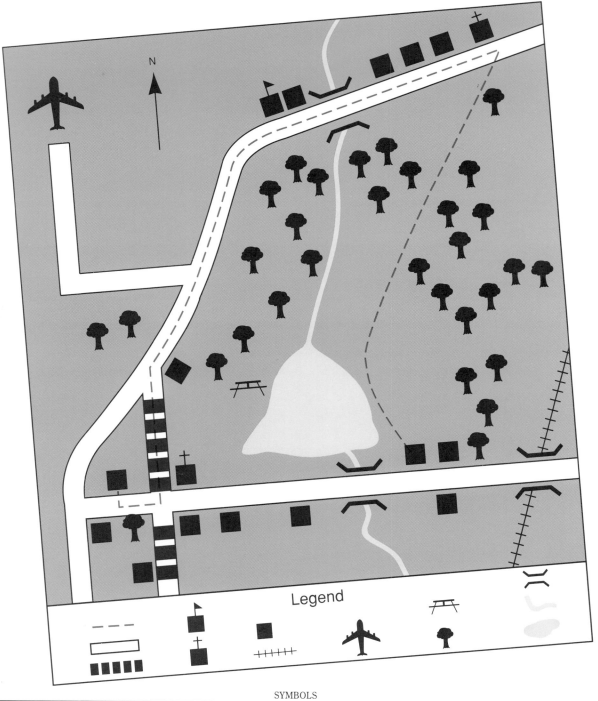

Legend

The Little Skunk's Path

A mother skunk and her young son live under a bridge, near a river. Early one morning, the young skunk got up with the sun and waddled out from under the bridge, while his mother was asleep. He was hungry, so he decided to look for something to eat. His path is shown on the map.

Some time later, the mother skunk awoke. She was alarmed that her son was gone. Fortunately, she could smell his scent. So the mother skunk set out to find her son. Use the legend, to describe in words, the path of the little skunk that the mother must follow.

The mother skunk knows that they will have to dodge cars in rush-hour traffic if they don't get home quickly. She wants to get her son home by the shortest route possible. Describe the way she should go, and what they will see on their way home.

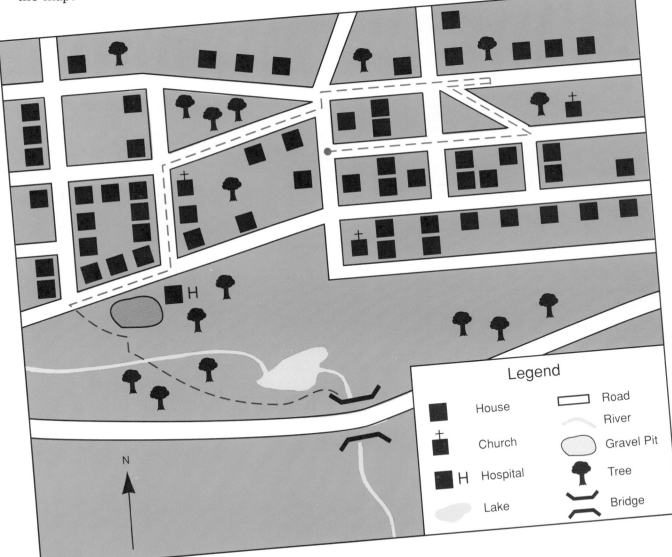

Colour as a Symbol 1

Jerry Davidson

This photograph shows some of Alberta's landscape. The town you see is Banff. Describe what you see.

This is a map of the same area but it shows only the different heights of the land, and the water. On this map, colour is being used as a symbol.

Legend

High Ground
Low Ground
Water

Colour as a Symbol 2

This photograph and map show part of Canada's Atlantic coastline. The map is not coloured. Redraw the map and colour it using blue for ocean, green for low ground and yellow for higher ground. Make a legend for your map.

The Shrinking School

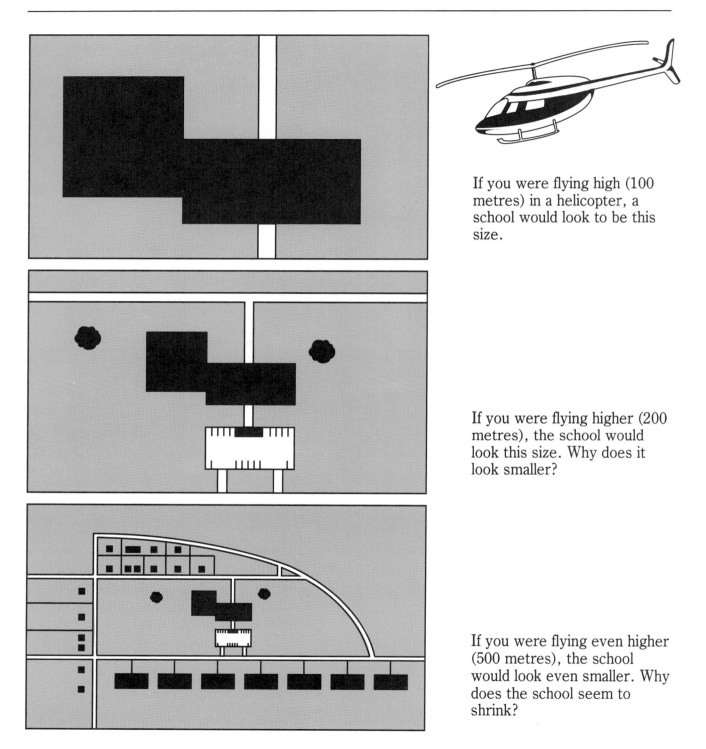

If you were flying high (100 metres) in a helicopter, a school would look to be this size.

If you were flying higher (200 metres), the school would look this size. Why does it look smaller?

If you were flying even higher (500 metres), the school would look even smaller. Why does the school seem to shrink?

Each drawing of the school is at a different scale. What does this mean?

Let's Make a Picture

Here is a drawing of a child's bedroom. Describe what you see.

Draw a picture of your own bedroom.

Let's Map the Classroom

Here is a drawing of a student's classroom. Describe what you see.

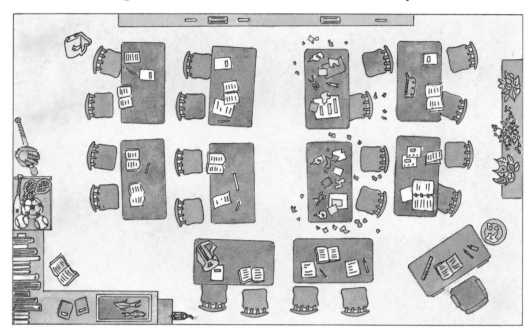

This is a map of the same classroom. Describe what you see.

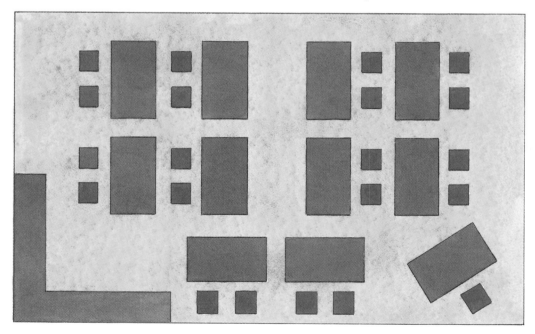

Now draw a map of your classroom.

Let's Map the School

Here is a map of a school. Can you find ways of drawing the rest of the map?

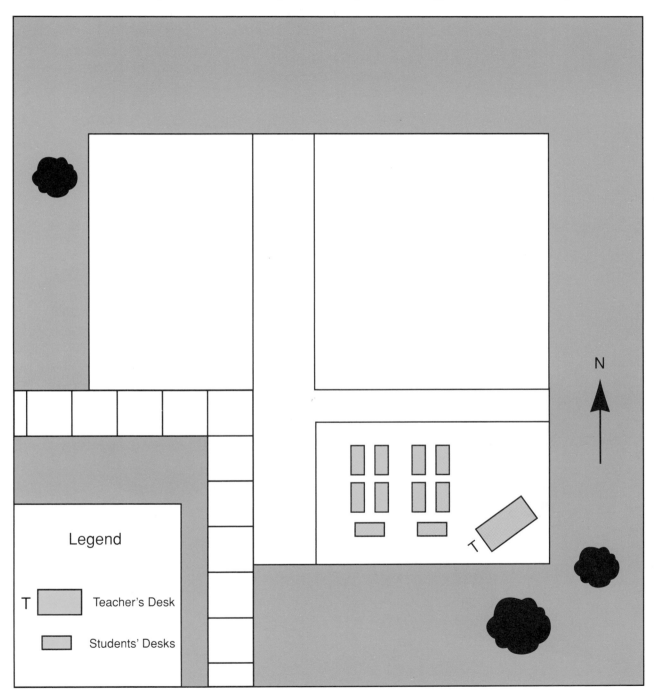

Make a map of your own school.

Location in the Classroom

Here is a photograph of three students in a classroom.

Can you see the arrow? It points out one girl sitting at her desk. This is her special place in the classroom. A word that describes her special place in the classroom is *location*.

Can you think of ways to describe this student's location?

Can you describe your own location in the classroom?

Birgitte Nielsen

Street Location

This photograph shows the location of Highgate Public School. The map also shows the location of the school.

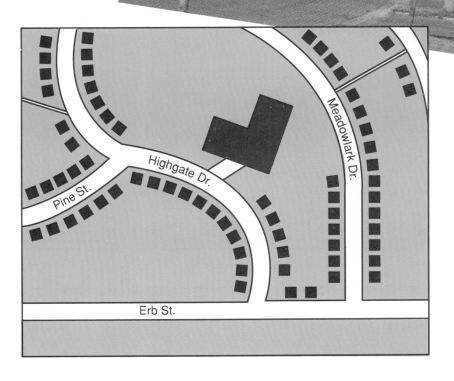

Birgitte Nielsen

1. How would you describe this school's location?
2. How would you describe the location of your own school? Draw a map to show it.
3. Describe the location of your home.

A Block of Buildings

This is a photograph of a block of buildings. Here the word *block* means the buildings between two streets.

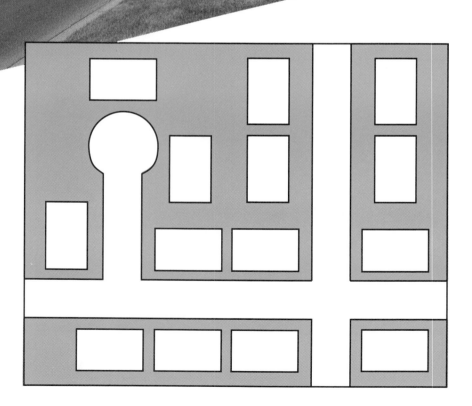

Birgitte Nielsen

This map is another way to show the same block.

1. What is different about one of the streets in this map?
2. Use a dictionary to find other meanings for the word *block*.

Map a Block

1. Choose a street between two cross streets.
2. Make chalk marks on the sidewalk even with the sides of each building.
3. Pace the distances between the marks.
4. Record these measurements in your notebook.
5. Map your measurements on graph paper or paper with large squares.

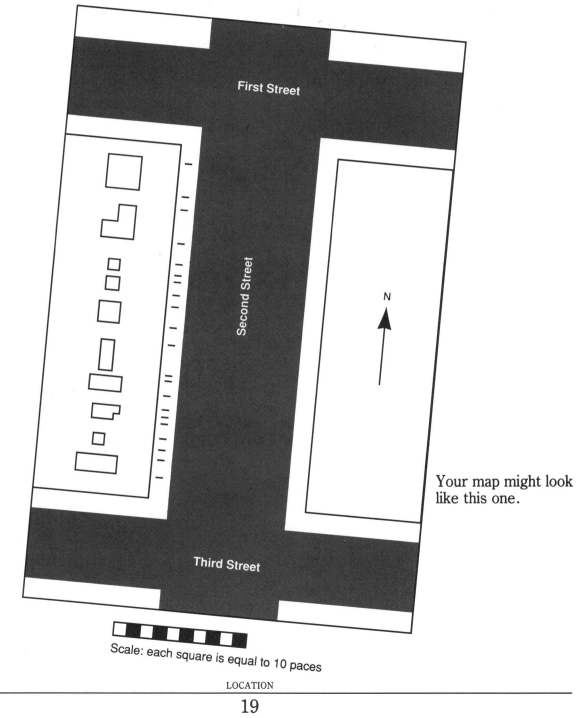

Your map might look like this one.

Scale: each square is equal to 10 paces

The Western Hemisphere

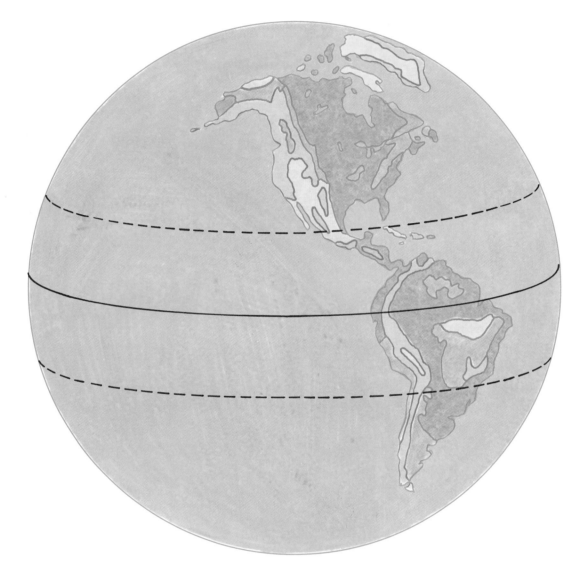

Legend

High Mountains
Low Mountains
High Ground
Low Ground
Water

Finding North

If your back is to the sun at midday, your shadow will point towards the north. Your right arm will point towards the east.

In which direction does your left arm point? In which direction is the sun?

Showing Directions

If your back is to the sun at midday, your shadow points towards the north. Your right arm points east. Your left arm points west. This drawing shows the directions without showing your shadow.

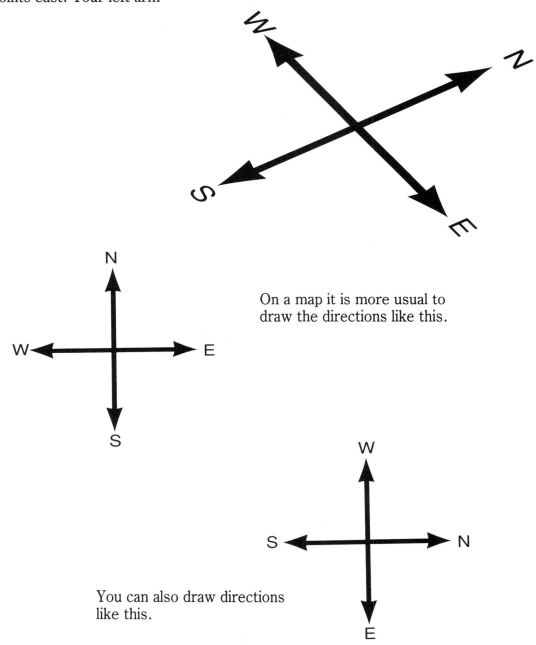

On a map it is more usual to draw the directions like this.

You can also draw directions like this.

Compass Directions

The four main directions of a compass are north, south, east and west. These four directions are called *cardinal points*.

Sometimes more directions are needed. This drawing shows the directions that are used most often.

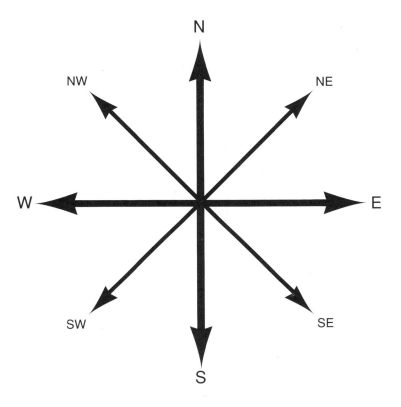

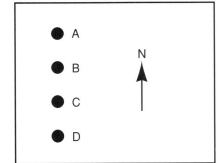

In which direction is A from B, D from C, A from C, and D from B?

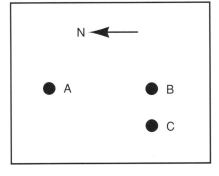

In which direction is A from B, A from C, C from A, and B from C?

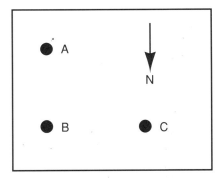

In which direction is A from B, A from C, C from A, and B from C?

Taking a Trip

1. Start at letter *A* and go to the airport by road. Describe what you see on your trip.

2. Start at letter *A* and walk to where the stream flows under the road. Describe what you see on your trip.

Legend

H Hospital	School	Park	Railroad	Picnic Area
House	Bridge	Gravel Road	Airport	Lake
Church		Gravel Pit		Road
				River

Finding Towns and Cities

It is often important to show the population of cities and towns on a map. This is done by using different shapes or sizes of symbols.

Here is a map of Southern Ontario. A large square is used to show Toronto. The circles show cities and towns which are smaller than Toronto.

Can you use an atlas to identify the other cities and towns on the map?

Southern Ontario

Legend

N

0   50   100   150km

Understanding Symbols

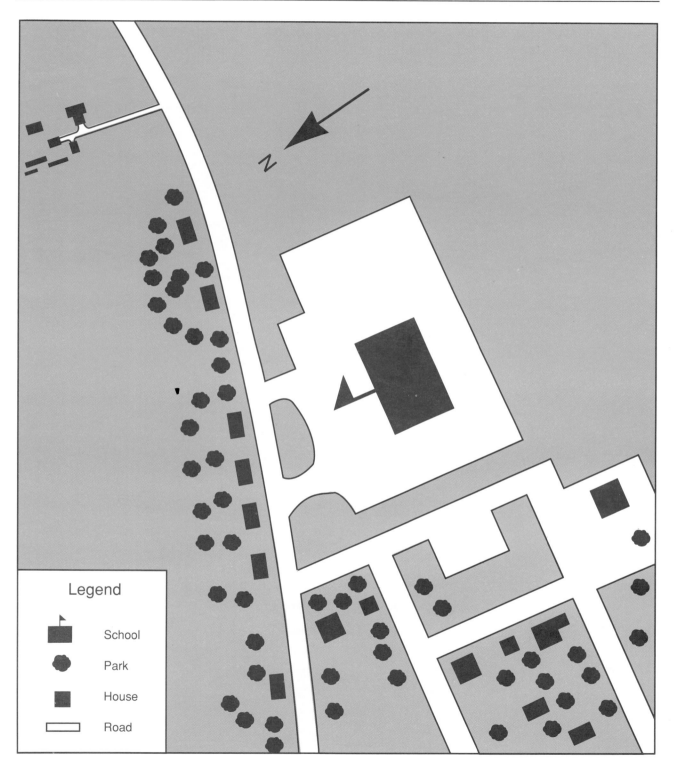

Legend

School

Park

House

Road

Using Colour 1

The drawing at the top of the page is a picture of an island. The bottom drawing is a relief map of that island. A relief map uses colours to show different heights of land.

How are the two drawings the same? How are they different?

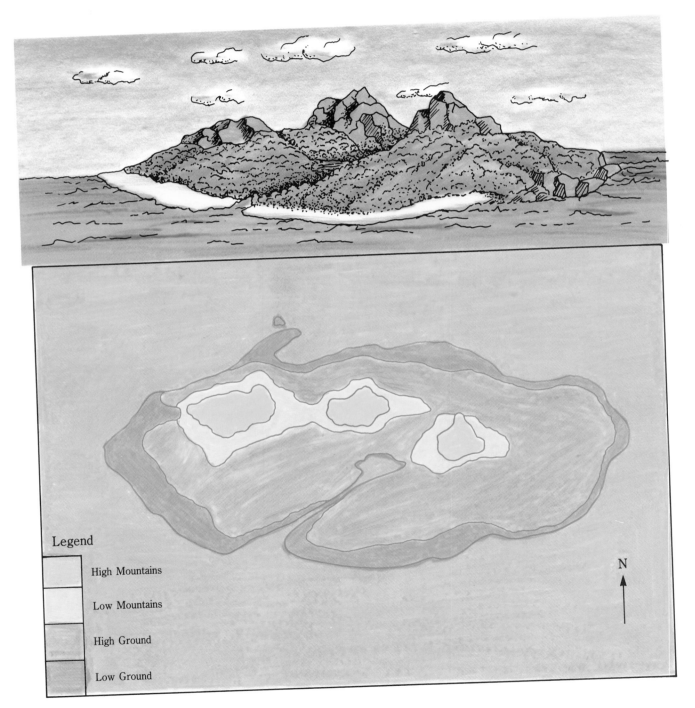

Legend

High Mountains

Low Mountains

High Ground

Low Ground

N

Using Colour 2

This map is like the one on page 28 but it is not the same. Can you tell how it is different? Draw a legend for this map.

Locate points A, B and C on the map. Which letter shows the highest point? Which letter shows the lowest point?

Can you describe what this island looks like?

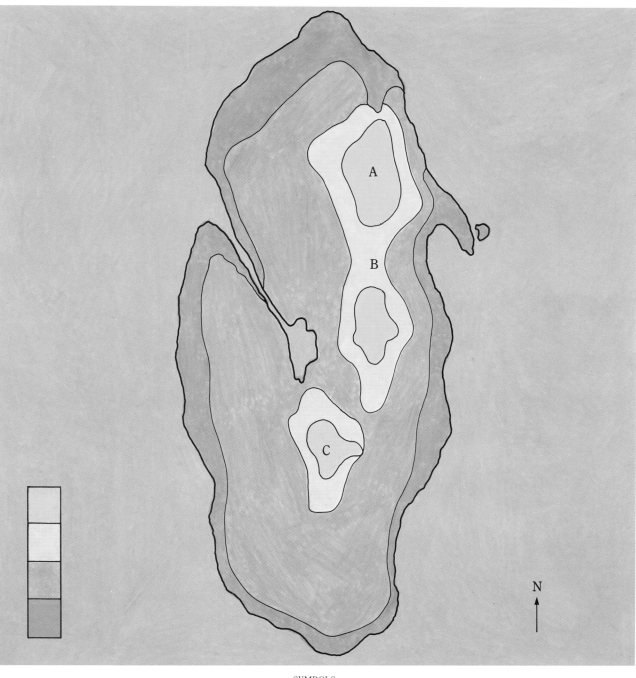

N

Island of Newfoundland

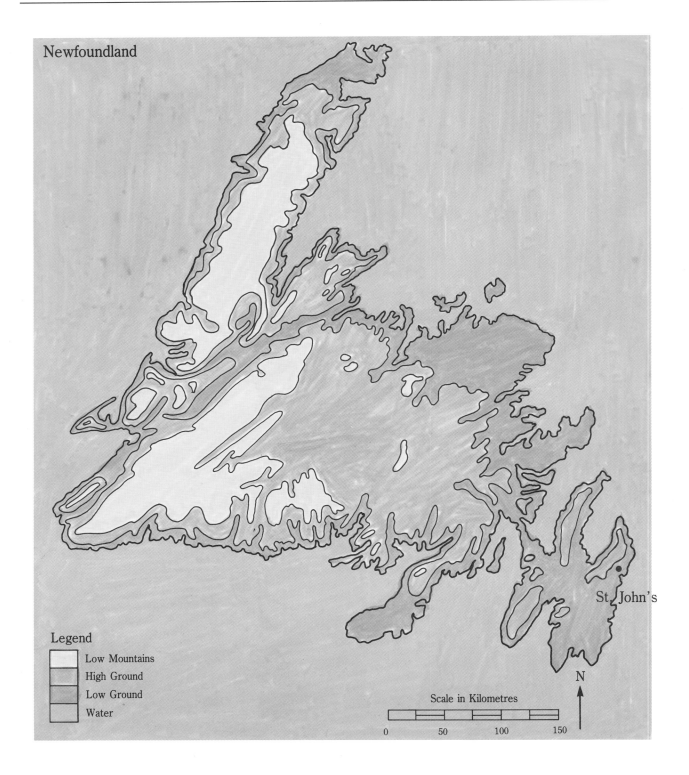

Newfoundland

St. John's

N

Legend

	Low Mountains
	High Ground
	Low Ground
	Water

Scale in Kilometres

0   50   100   150

Measuring Trees

Measure how tall the tree is in this picture. How tall is the real tree?

To decide how tall the real tree is you need more information.

Measure how tall the tree is in this picture. Measure the person in the picture.

How many times taller than the person is the tree? How tall is the real tree?

To decide how tall the real tree is you need more information.

SCALE

31

Measure how tall the tree is in this picture. This is the same person. Measure the person. How many times taller than the person is the tree?

B

Which tree is taller — A or B? How tall is the real tree?

If the person is two metres tall, how tall is tree A? How tall is tree B?

Scale and Distance

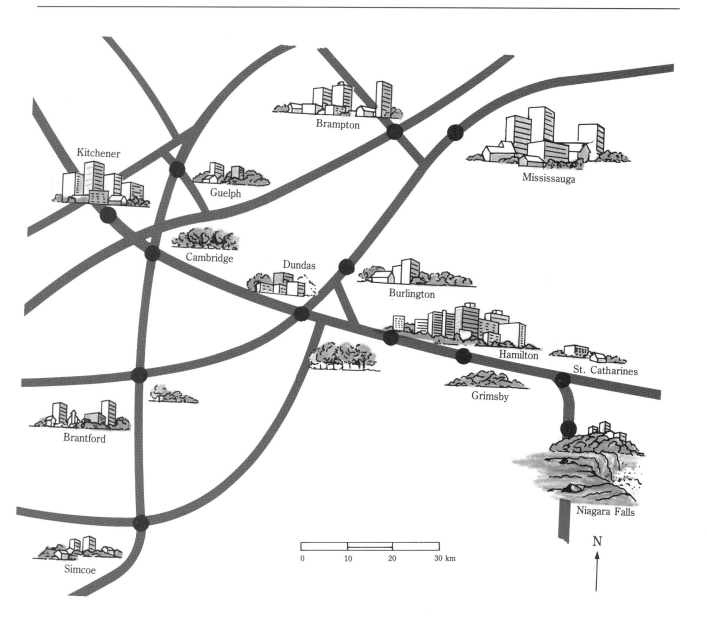

1. Use the scale on the map to estimate how far Dundas is from Hamilton, Brantford is from Mississauga, and Cambridge is from Brampton.

2. Which is further, Dundas to Brantford, or Dundas to Burlington?

3. If you are travelling in a car at a speed of 100 kilometres per hour, approximately how long will it take to drive from Niagara Falls to Brampton, Simcoe to Burlington, and Kitchener to Guelph?

Meeting Place

Here is a map of part of a city.

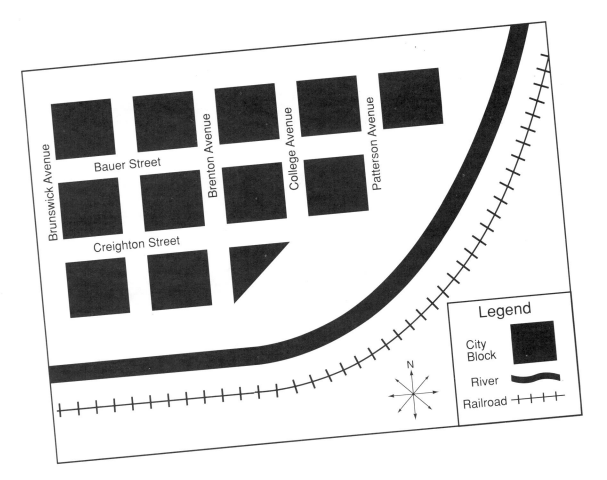

1. Imagine you are somewhere on the map. How can you describe where you are to me?

2. What must you know if you want me to meet you at a specific place? What would you say to me?

3. How many streets must you know before you can locate a certain place on one street?

4. How many streets must you know before you can locate a certain place on a street corner?

5. Suppose you are standing on a very busy corner. There are many people and there is a lot of traffic. How could we be sure of meeting one another?

A Grid Map

This is a map with a grid drawn on it. A grid makes it easier to find places on a map.

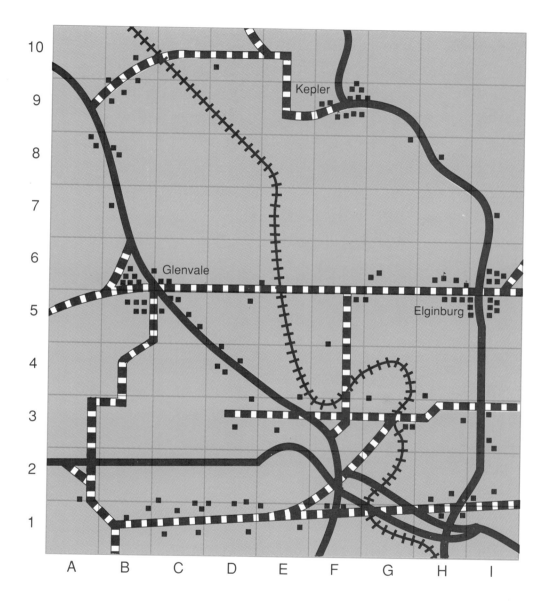

1. Describe what you see on the map. Do you understand all the symbols?
2. In which square is the town of Kepler located?
3. In which squares is the town of Elginburg located?
4. What is in squares B5, G4, A9 and F3?
5. Through what squares do you pass to get from Elginburg to Kepler?

Leslie's Neighbourhood

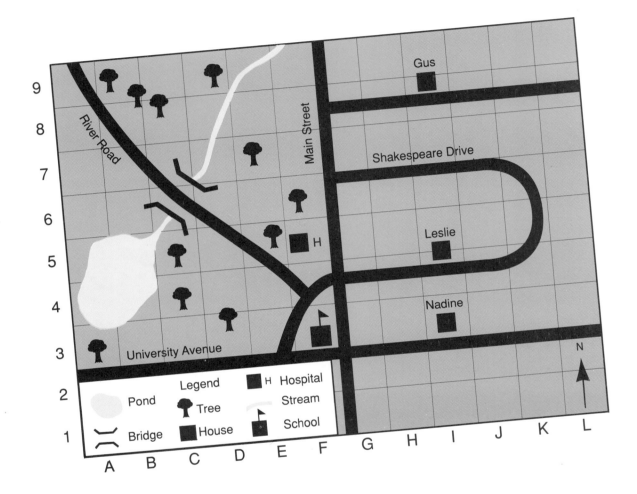

1. Who lives closest to the school?

2. Who lives furthest from the hospital?

3. In which direction is the pond from Leslie's house?

4. What is located in square F5?

The Saint John Region

Use this grid map of the Saint John, New Brunswick region to practise locating places.

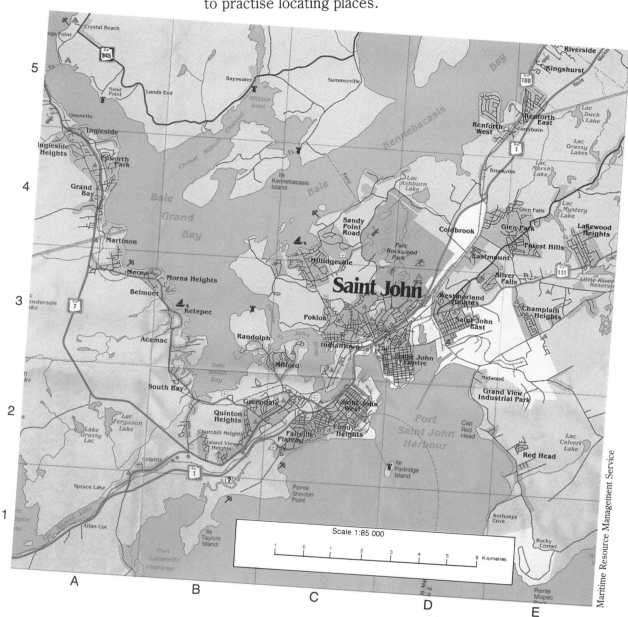

Maritime Resource Management Service

1. Which suburbs of Saint John are located in squares B2, E3 and A4?

2. What is the location of Saint John Centre, Duck Lake and Sheldon Point?

3. If you sailed from Crystal Beach to Partridge Island, through which squares would you pass?

A Sketch Map

Jerry Davidson

This is an aerial photograph of downtown Vancouver, British Columbia.

Maps are often made from aerial photographs. This is a sketch map of downtown Vancouver.

How are the photograph and the map different from each other?

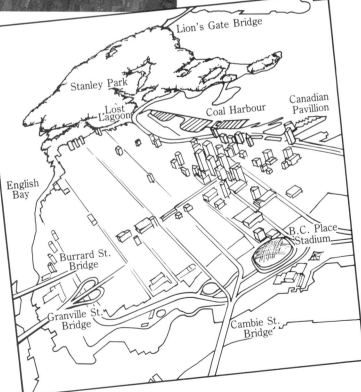

Lion's Gate Bridge

Stanley Park

Lost Lagoon

Coal Harbour

Canadian Pavillion

English Bay

B.C. Place Stadium

Burrard St. Bridge

Granville St. Bridge

Cambie St. Bridge

A Different View

This aerial photograph and map show two views of the Parliament Buildings in Ottawa, Canada.

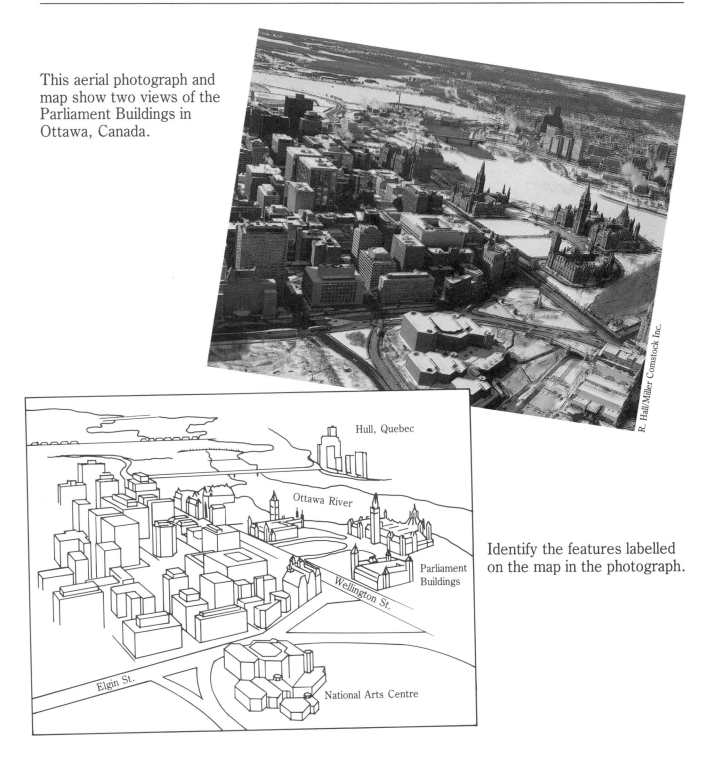

R. Hall/Miller Comstock Inc.

Hull, Quebec

Ottawa River

Parliament Buildings

Wellington St.

Elgin St.

National Arts Centre

Identify the features labelled on the map in the photograph.

Night and Day

Which circles represent day? Which circles represent night? Why are there two black circles?

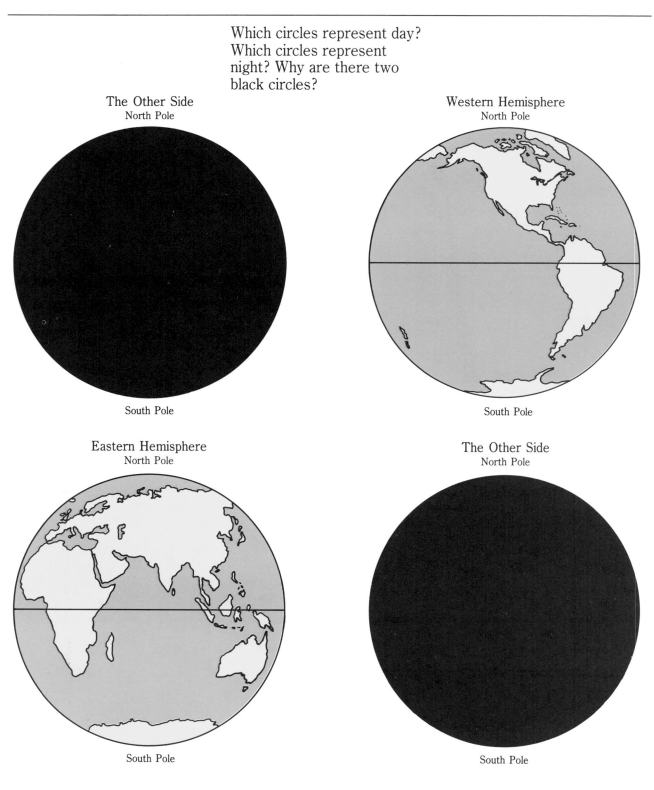

The Other Side
North Pole

South Pole

Western Hemisphere
North Pole

South Pole

Eastern Hemisphere
North Pole

South Pole

The Other Side
North Pole

South Pole

What Is Time?

What is time? You might think of time as every moment there has ever been or ever will be. The passing hours, days, weeks, months and years are based on astronomical periods. *Astronomy* is a science that studies the planets and stars.

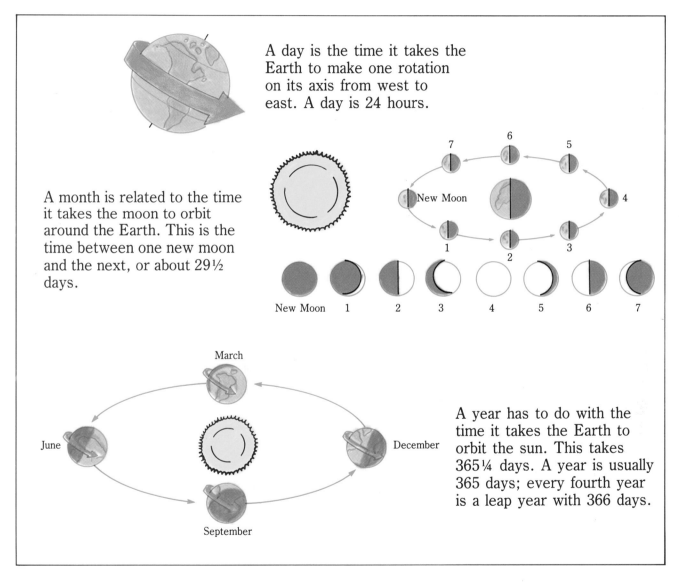

A day is the time it takes the Earth to make one rotation on its axis from west to east. A day is 24 hours.

A month is related to the time it takes the moon to orbit around the Earth. This is the time between one new moon and the next, or about 29½ days.

New Moon   1   2   3   4   5   6   7

A year has to do with the time it takes the Earth to orbit the sun. This takes 365¼ days. A year is usually 365 days; every fourth year is a leap year with 366 days.

1. How many hours are there in a day? a week? a month? a year?

2. What is a leap year? What day is the extra day? What years from now to the year 2000 will be leap years?

3. Why can't you see a new moon?

The Eastern Hemisphere

Legend

High Mountains
Low Mountains
High Ground
Low Ground
Water

The Globe

1. Can you locate all the continents and oceans listed in the legend? Label them on a map of the world.

2. Which continents and oceans are in the Eastern Hemisphere?

3. Which continents and oceans are in the Western Hemisphere?

Legend

North America
South America
Asia
Africa
Australia
Europe
Pacific Ocean
Atlantic Ocean
Indian Ocean
Antarctic Ocean
Arctic Ocean

Canada in North America

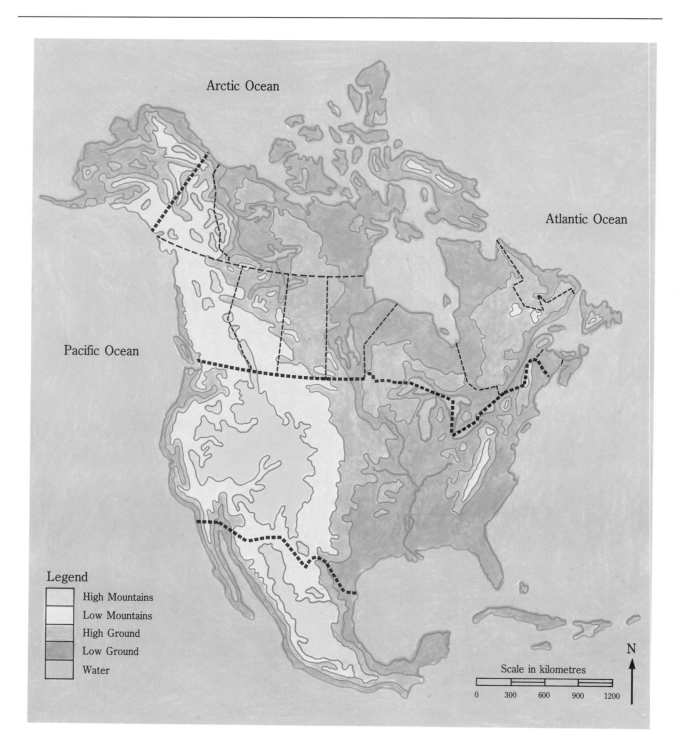

Arctic Ocean

Atlantic Ocean

Pacific Ocean

Legend

	High Mountains
	Low Mountains
	High Ground
	Low Ground
	Water

Scale in kilometres

0   300   600   900   1200

N

A Highway Map

When you travel from one place to another, you need to know two things — the direction and the distance. When people travel to familiar places they understand which direction to go in and how far to go. What do people do when they travel to new places?

When people travel in another province or country they usually need help. They need information about directions and distances. A highway map is one place to get this information.

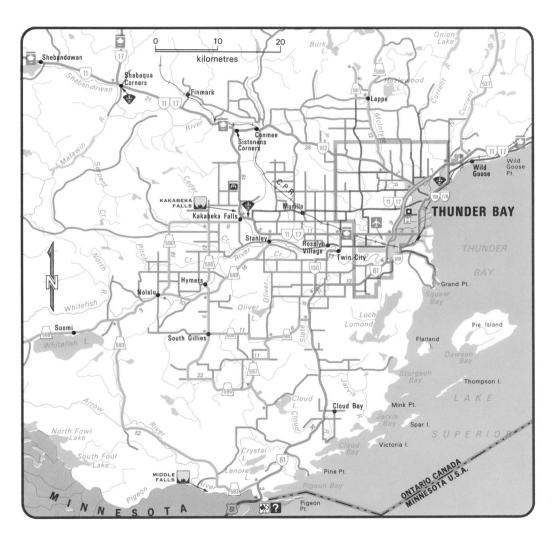

1. How many different kinds of roads are shown on this map?

2. Describe how you would get to Middle Falls Provincial Park from Thunder Bay. In which direction would you be travelling?

3. How far is it from Thunder Bay to Shabaqua Corners?

Making a Map

This is a map of an imaginary island called Gull Island. As the following description shows, this map is not finished. Draw the map in your notebook and complete it.

Mt. Adanac is an old volcano. It is 450 metres high. You can see all of Windy Harbour and most of the ocean around the island from a lighthouse, represented by the symbol ▲

There is a lake in the north-eastern part of the island. A slow, winding river flows from the lake to the east end of the harbour. At the most southern part of Windy Harbour, there is a small settlement called Mapleton.

The southwest tip of the island is called Caribou Point. From here, a paved road runs east along the coast and then

north to Mapleton. The road follows the harbour until it crosses the river and then goes northwest until it reaches a point 20 kilometres from Mt. Adanac. A farm is located 10 kilometres south-west of the end of this road. The farm is reached by a gravel road.

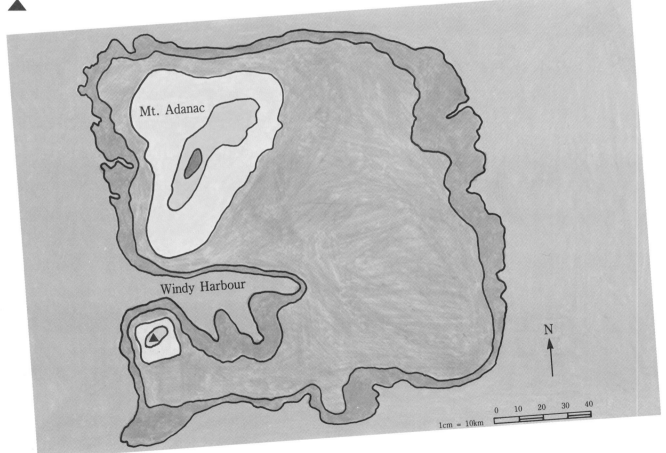

1. Make a legend to show symbols for things that are in the description.

2. From the lighthouse can you see Mapleton? the farm? the lake?

Colours and Contours

Cartographers use the word *relief* to describe the height of the land. Colour is often used as a symbol to show relief.

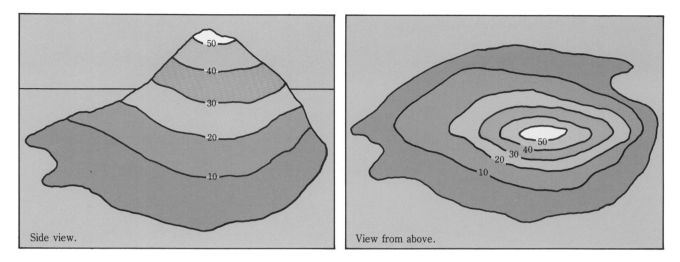

Side view.

View from above.

At times, only the lines are used to show the height of the land. These lines are called *contour lines*. A contour line shows land at the same height.

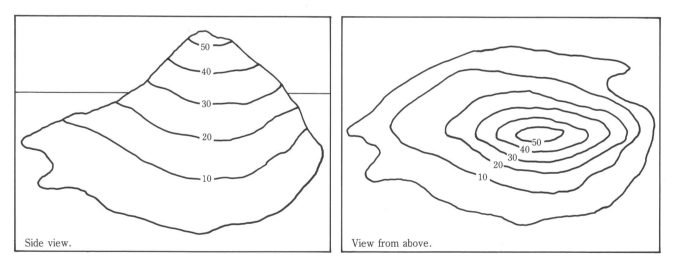

Side view.

View from above.

Use different colours of plasticine to build the hill shown in the drawings on the left. Put a piece of paper between each colour. When the hill is finished, cut the papers to follow the shape of the hill. Remove the pieces of paper from the hill. Place each piece of paper on top of the one below. The shapes of the pieces of paper should look like the drawings on the right.

Parts of a Topographic Map

Different maps have different uses. A *topographic map* shows a small area in great detail. The scale is therefore quite large. There are many important parts of a topographic map — scale, direction, symbols, colours and contours.

REGINA SASKATCHEWAN

1. How is each important part of a topographic map shown?

2. What important part of a map is missing from this map? How would it be shown?

A Pictograph

A graph is one way to show information. When picture symbols are used, the graph is called a *pictograph*.

In the following pictograph, the symbol is a __________. The pictograph shows how many years the average person spends eating, bathing, sleeping, watching television and working, before retiring at 65 years of age.

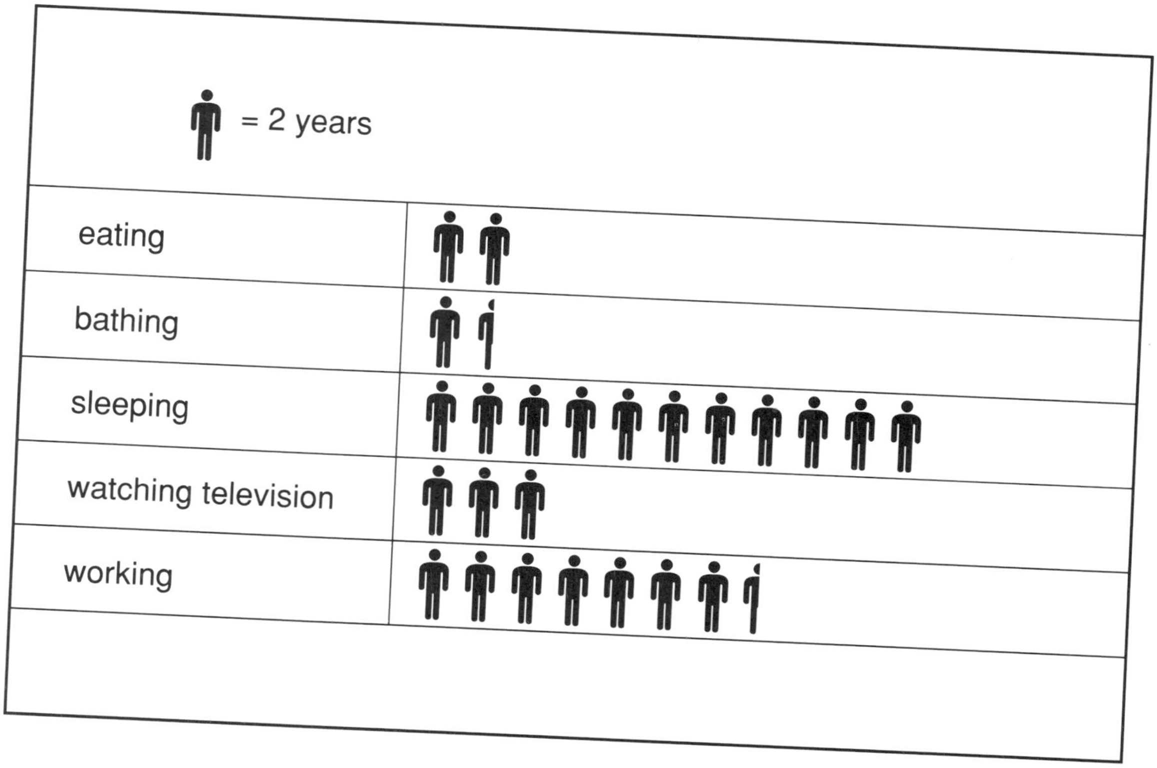

How many years will each of us spend eating and watching television before retiring?

Draw a pictograph to show the life span of animals in captivity. Here is a chart of eight animals and their life spans from which to draw your pictograph. (In the wild, each animal's life span is rarely as long.)

Animals	*Life Span in Years*
beaver	5
chipmunk	6
cow	15
dog	12
gorilla	20
hippopotamus	25
horse	20
mouse	3

Which animal has the longest life span, and which has the shortest?

A Bar Graph

Information that can be shown on a pictograph can usually be shown on a bar graph too. The following bar graph uses bars to show the same information as the pictograph on page 49, about the number of years the average person spends doing certain things, before retiring at 65 years of age.

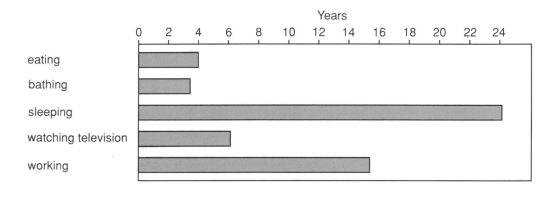

How many years will each of us spend bathing, sleeping and working before retiring?

The following bar graph shows when babies learn to do certain things, like roll over. No two babies are ever alike, nor do they learn to do things at exactly the same time. Some babies walk well by eleven months, others walk well by fifteen months.

The coloured section on the bar graph shows the age range for learning a variety of activities.

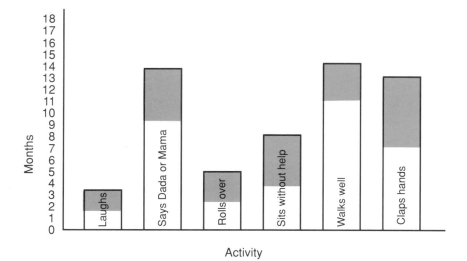

What age range does the bar graph show for each activity?

A Line Graph

A line graph shows change. It uses a line to show how things increase or decrease. A line which rises from left to right shows an increase. A line which falls from left to right shows a decrease.

The Consumer Price Index keeps track of changes in the prices of such common requirements as food, shelter, clothing, transportation and recreation. The price index doesn't indicate actual price levels. It measures movements from an assigned period, presently 1981, which is given a value of 100.

This graph shows how the cost of living in Canada changed from 1977 to 1987.

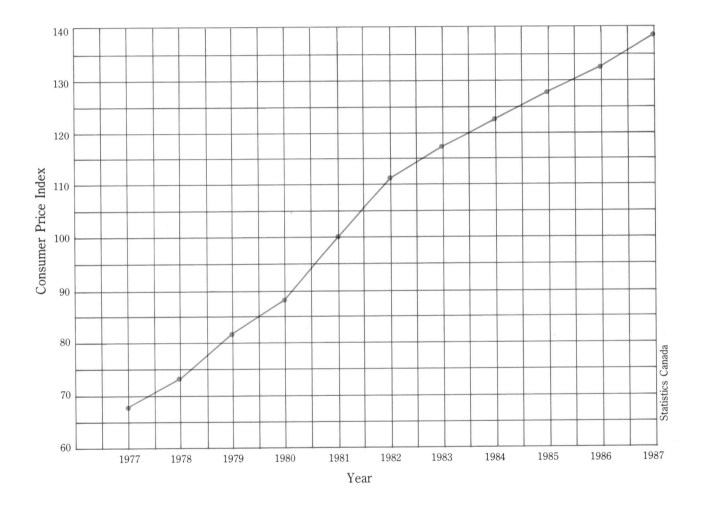

1. What was the Consumer Price Index for 1977?

2. What was the Consumer Price Index for 1987?

3. Did the cost of living in Canada increase or decrease from 1977 to 1987?

Making Things Smaller

It would be impossible to draw maps if you had to draw things their real size. No actual place is small enough to fit on a piece of paper. Scale makes it possible to draw maps. You can draw a smaller version of the real thing. The scale used to draw a map should appear somewhere on the map.

Here are two drawings of the Canadian flag. The second flag is a scaled-down version of the first. This shows one way of drawing to scale. Each square in the smaller drawing is smaller than each square in the larger drawing. A scaled-down version is made by drawing the flag in exactly the same position in the smaller squares.

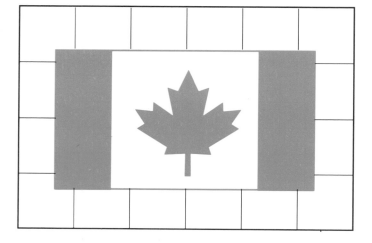

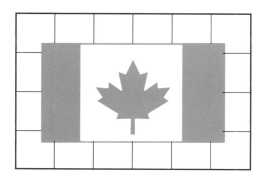

Make scaled-down versions of the following drawings.

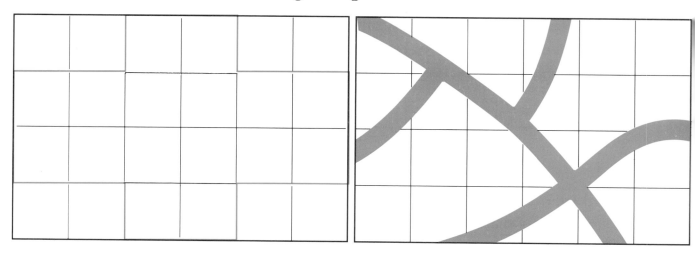

Using Scale 1

This map shows several towns and cities in the province of Alberta.

The map is a scaled-down version of Alberta. Every centimetre on the map stands

for 84 kilometres of Alberta. This information is shown on the scale.

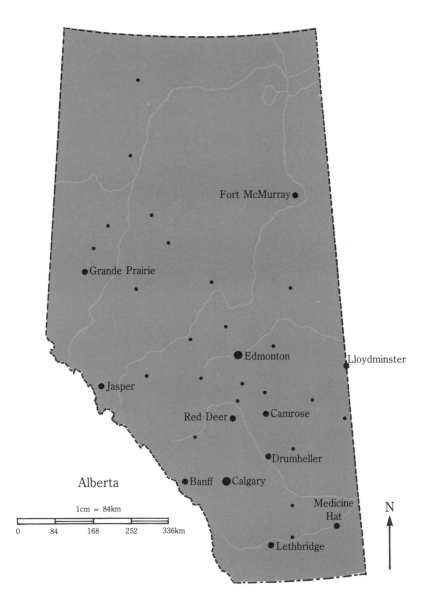

Fort McMurray●

●Grande Prairie

●Edmonton

Lloydminster
●

●Jasper

Red Deer● ●Camrose

●Drumheller

Alberta

●Banff ●Calgary

1cm = 84km

Medicine
Hat
●

N

0   84   168   252   336km

●Lethbridge

1. In centimetres, measure the distances between Edmonton and the other places on the map.

2. Use the scale to determine how far Edmonton is from each town or city labelled on the map.

Using Scale 2

On page 53 there is a map of Alberta. Edmonton is shown as one place within the province. On this page Edmonton is shown in much more detail. This is possible because the map on this page is drawn to a larger scale than the map of Alberta.

THE CITY OF EDMONTON

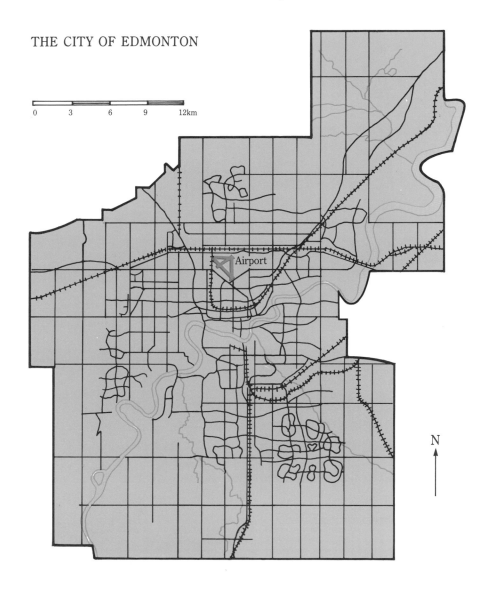

1. What does one centimetre stand for in the map of Alberta on page 53? in the map of Edmonton on this page?

2. Measure the size of the airport. Use a larger scale to make a larger drawing of this area.

3. Does the map of the province or the map of the city show the greater land area? show the greater detail? use the larger scale?

A Grid Map of Fredericton

The grid map on this page shows part of the city of Fredericton, New Brunswick.

1 City Hall
2 Soldiers Barracks
3 Lord Beaverbrook Statue
4 Provincial Government Offices
5 Boyce Farmers' Market
6 Old Burial Ground
7 Old Government House
8 Harness Racing Track
9 York Railway Station
10 University of New Brunswick

metres

1. What is the street location of the Fredericton City Hall?

2. What is located in square H7?

3. Give the grid coordinates for the Harness Racing Track and the York Railway Station.

4. In which squares is the University of New Brunswick located?

Highways in the Yukon

Government of Yukon

1. What highway would you take from Whitehorse to Pelly Crossing? What towns would you pass through?

2. How many kilometres is it from Beaver Creek to Haines Junction? Skagway to Carcross? Teslin to Little Salmon?

3. Give someone written directions telling them how to go from Destruction Bay to Ross by car. Give directions and distances.

Using a Topographic Map

The pattern of small squares on a topographic map is called a grid. A grid on a topographic map is useful for determining location.

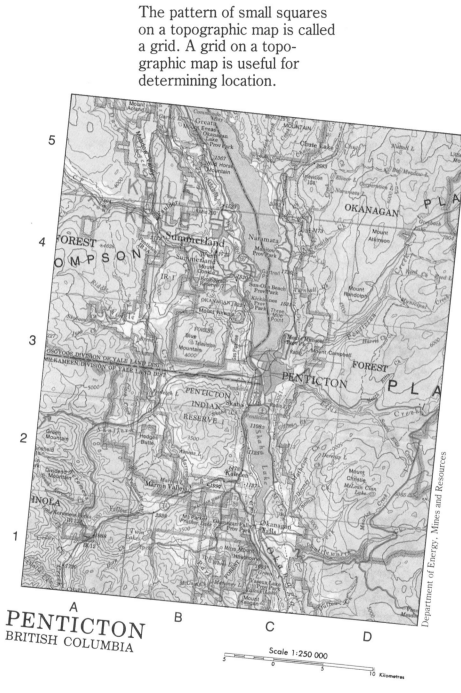

PENTICTON
BRITISH COLUMBIA

Scale 1:250 000

10 Kilometres

1. What is the location of Penticton? Okanagan Falls? Summerland?

2. Describe the features in squares B3 and B5.

Canadian Standard Time Zones

This map shows the number and the location of the time zones in Canada.

There is only a 30 minute time difference between Newfoundland time and Atlantic time.

In Saskatchewan, the clocks do not change for daylight-saving time as they do in the rest of the country. Daylight-saving time is one hour in advance of standard time and gives more daylight in the evening. Clocks are set ahead one hour in the spring and back one hour in the fall.

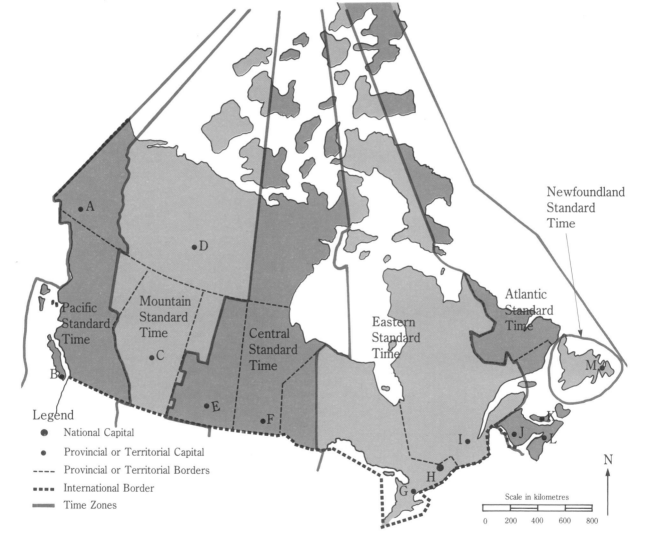

1. Name the 13 cities shown on the map (A to M).

2. If it is noon in Ottawa, what time is it in each of the Canadian cities shown on the map?

Maps and Globes

To make a map of the world you must show something that is round in a way that is flat. This is a problem for cartographers. It is not possible to make an accurate world map. All flat maps have some distortion. Either the sizes of the continents are not right or their shapes are wrong. The distances and directions can also be incorrect. This world map is commonly used even though it is not as correct as a global representation.

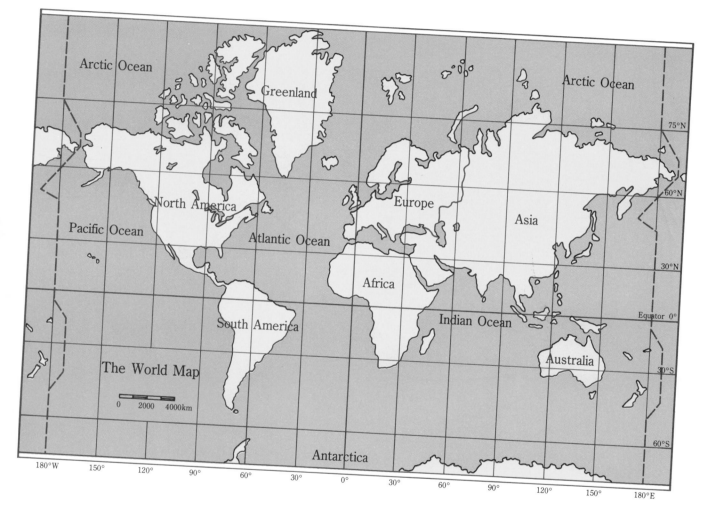

A Flat Map

Flat maps of the world are often used as a way to show information. For example, the following map shows the exploration routes taken by six world explorers. These explorers were among the earliest Europeans to explore the Canadian coastlines. It would be difficult to show this kind of information on a globe.

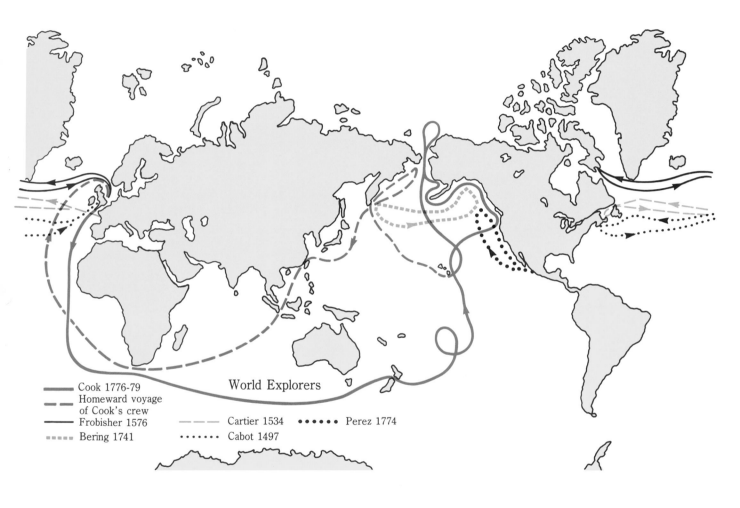

World Explorers

—— Cook 1776-79
– – – Homeward voyage
of Cook's crew
—— Frobisher 1576
▪▪▪▪ Bering 1741

– – – Cartier 1534   •••••• Perez 1774
•••• Cabot 1497

1. Name the six explorers.

2. Describe the route of one explorer in terms of continents and oceans.

3. Use string and tape to trace one explorer's route on a globe.

Let's Go Orienteering

Directions can be shown on a map in several ways:

- by using a north arrow;
- by showing the four cardinal points (N,E,W,S);
- by using the compass rose which shows eight direction points (the long points show the four cardinal directions).

A *compass* is a tool to show direction based on the compass rose. The compass is used as a tool in the sport of orienteering. In orienteering, people are given distance and direction clues to travel between points on a set course.

A compass is also used during searches for people who are lost or who have been involved in an accident. For instance, a ski patrol located in Banff may be sent out when people are trapped by a snowslide or when there has been a skiing accident.

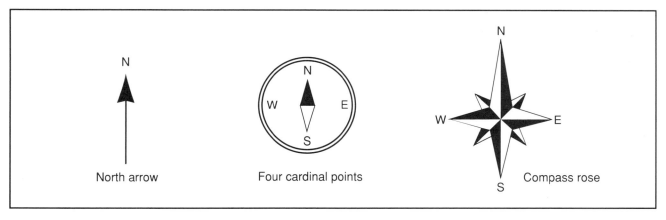

North arrow   Four cardinal points   Compass rose

When you hold a compass you orient something to yourself.

1. What happens if the person in this picture changes position?

2. Describe what would happen to the directions if the person moved to the other side of the gate.

3. Use a compass to find north. This is called "setting a compass."

4. Find the directions of various parts of your classroom.

5. Move outside and find the directions of several objects.

Landmarks

Landmarks are objects that stand out in the landscape. People often use landmarks to orient themselves if they become lost. Outside cities landmarks may be natural or artificial. In cities they are usually artificial.

These photographs show landmarks in Canadian cities.

The Calgary Olympic Saddledome and the Calgary Tower

Calgary Tourist and Convention Bureau

The CN Tower

Photo provided courtesy CN Tower

The Chateau Frontenac

Ministère du Tourisme du Québec

The Halifax Citadel

Nova Scotia Tourism

1. What do these landmarks have in common?

2. Identify two landmarks in your own community.

3. Describe your route home from school by using your own personal landmarks.

Pictorial Symbols

Some symbols look like what they represent and others do not. Symbols that resemble what they represent are called *pictorial symbols*.

Which symbols on the maps, chart and graph below look like what they represent?

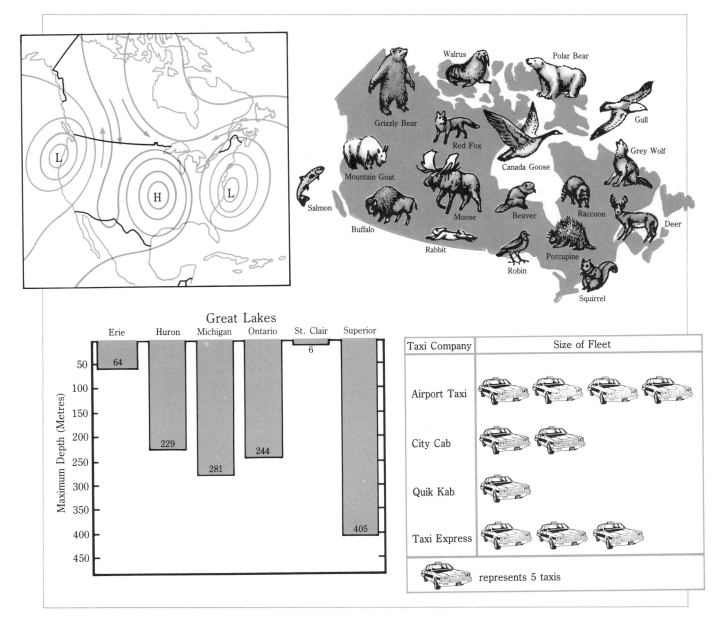

Great Lakes

Maximum Depth (Metres)

Erie	Huron	Michigan	Ontario	St. Clair	Superior
64	229	281	244	6	405

Taxi Company	Size of Fleet
Airport Taxi	
City Cab	
Quik Kab	
Taxi Express	

represents 5 taxis

Use an atlas to find pages where pictorial symbols are used to show information.

Temperature Line Graphs

On this page, line graphs are used to show the annual temperatures of four Canadian places. To discover the average temperature for a particular month, find the point where a line from the month meets the line on the graph. Read the number at the left-hand side of the graph.

The dashed line on the graph represents a temperature of 5.6°C. This is the temperature at which plant growth occurs. The length of the growing season is shown by that part of the graph which is above the dashed line.

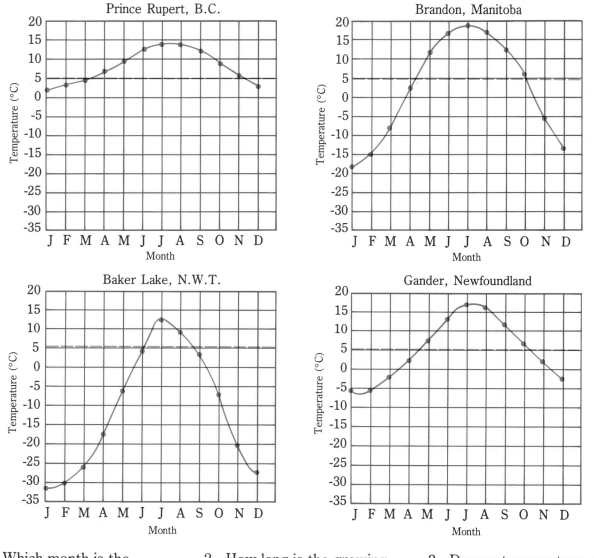

1. Which month is the warmest for each place above? Which is the coldest?

2. How long is the growing season for each place?

3. Draw a temperature graph for your community.

Precipitation Bar Graphs

A bar graph is often used to show precipitation. On this map of Canada, bar graphs show the annual precipitation of cities across Canada. Rainfall is shown in blue and snowfall is shown in white.

A bar graph can be constructed either vertically or horizontally. Which way are the bars on these precipitation graphs drawn?

A Circle Graph

Some information is best shown on a circle graph, especially if a graph is to show fractions or parts of a whole.

Canada's forests make up 44 percent of the country's total land area. The federal and provincial governments periodically take an inventory of the national forests. The circle graph on this page shows how the whole inventory is divided among the provinces and territories.

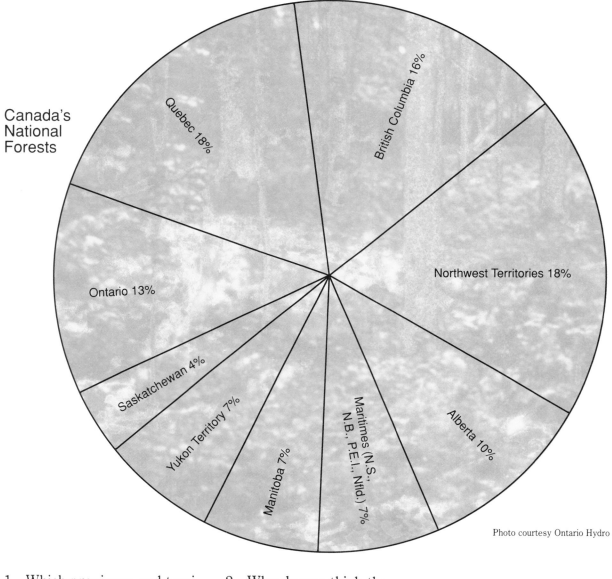

Canada's National Forests

British Columbia 16%

Quebec 18%

Northwest Territories 18%

Ontario 13%

Saskatchewan 4%

Yukon Territory 7%

Manitoba 7%

Maritimes (N.S., N.B., P.E.I., Nfld.) 7%

Alberta 10%

Photo courtesy Ontario Hydro

1. Which provinces and territories have the largest percentages of national forests?

2. Why do you think the Maritime provinces have a small percentage of national forests?

SYMBOLS

66

Canada's Population Growth

This line graph shows information about the growth of Canada's population from 1871 to 1986. Starting with 1871, the figures are given every ten years to 1981. These were years when Canada's census was taken.

A *census* is an official count of the people in a country. The figure shown for 1986 is an estimate for that year.

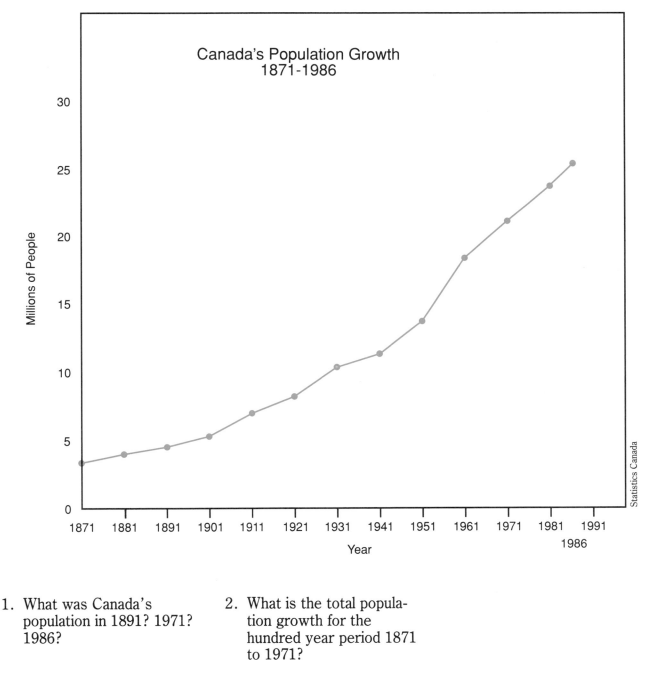

Canada's Population Growth
1871-1986

Millions of People

Year

1986

Statistics Canada

1. What was Canada's population in 1891? 1971? 1986?

2. What is the total population growth for the hundred year period 1871 to 1971?

Sketch Maps 1

A *sketch map* is a drawing which shows the important parts of a landscape. This kind of map is used to record information.

Sketch maps are often made from photographs so the map can be drawn the same size as the photograph. Make your own sketch map from the photograph below.

An aerial photograph of Montreal, Quebec.

Relations Publiques, Ville de Montréal

The beginning of a sketch map of Montreal, Quebec.

1. Identify the features in the photograph which appear in this sketch map.

2. Identify other features in the photograph that could be shown in a sketch map.

Sketch Maps 2

This aerial photograph shows the agricultural centre of North Battleford, Saskatchewan. The partial sketch map below shows several features from the photograph. Copy and complete the sketch map in your notebook.

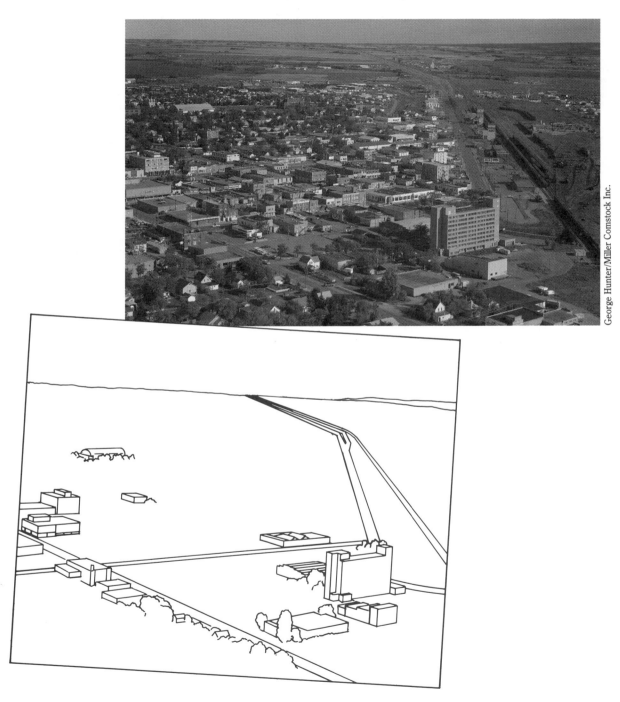

George Hunter/Miller Comstock Inc.

Sketch Maps 3

Practise drawing sketch maps
from the two aerial
photographs on this page.

Saskatoon,
Saskatchewan.

Jerry Davidson

Grand Manan Island,
New Brunswick.

New Brunswick Dept. of Tourism

Using a Grid for Location

Parallels of latitude and meridians of longitude make a grid. A grid is used to locate different places.

1. Which town's location is D3? B5?

2. What is the location of Spy Hill? Seaport? Steeltown?

3. Through which squares would you pass if you sailed in a boat from Sandy Bay to Rocky Cove?

Latitude is the distance north or south of the equator, and is measured in degrees. Latitude lines are called parallels because they are parallel to the Equator. The latitude of Ottawa is 45°N.

Longitude is the distance east or west of the Prime Meridian, and is measured in degrees. Lines of longitude are called meridians. The longitude of Ottawa is 74° W.

The location of Ottawa is 45°N, 74°W. Note that latitude is given before longitude and both are measured in degrees.

Locating Places

This map indicates some of
the important cities in the
Eastern Hemisphere.

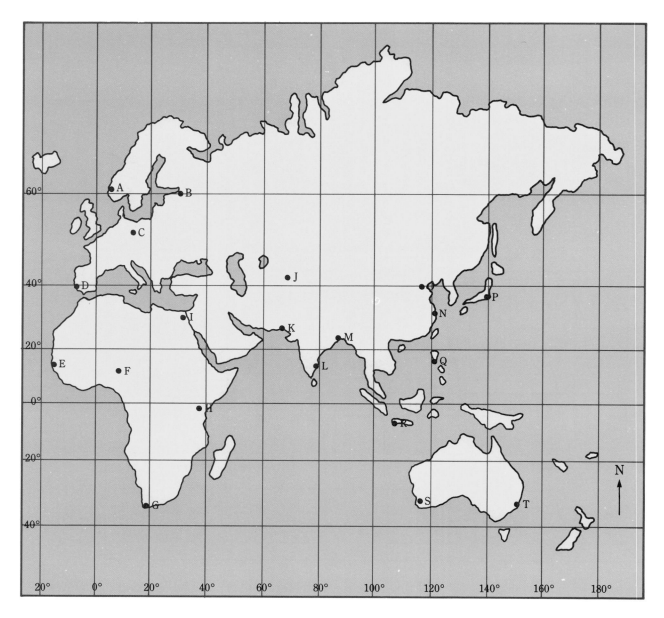

1. As accurately as possible,
   identify the location of
   each letter on the map.

2. Look up each city in an
   atlas or gazetteer to find
   its latitude and longitude.

3. Match the letters and the
   cities.

Time Lines

A *time line* is a graph which shows important events in the order in which they happened. It also shows how the events are related to one another.

A.
Here is a time line for a fourteen-year-old boy named Tomas. Each square stands for one year in his life.

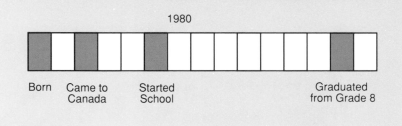

1980

Born · Came to Canada · Started School · Graduated from Grade 8

1. When was Tomas born?

2. What year did Tomas start school? How old was he?

3. What year did Tomas graduate from grade eight? How old was he?

4. Which square shows when he was nine?

5. Make a time line to show some important events in your life. On the time line, write the year each event took place.

B.
Here is an example of a Canadian historical time line that indicates the years the provinces and territories joined Confederation.

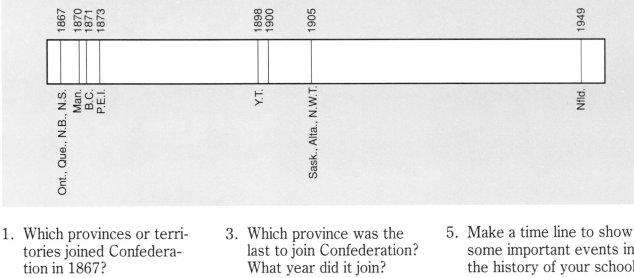

1867 1870 1871 1873 · 1898 1900 · 1905 · 1949

Ont., Que., N.B., N.S. · Man. · B.C. · P.E.I. · Y.T. · Sask., Alta., N.W.T. · Nfld.

1. Which provinces or territories joined Confederation in 1867?

2. How many provinces or territories joined Confederation in 1905?

3. Which province was the last to join Confederation? What year did it join?

4. What year did your province or territory join Confederation?

5. Make a time line to show some important events in the history of your school, city or town.

TIME

The Shrinking Globe

The amount of time it took explorers to sail the oceans did not change very much for many centuries. In the last century, it has taken less time to travel between continents. Travelling time has decreased as new inventions improve the ways people travel.

Because it takes less time to travel between continents, some people say the globe is shrinking.

Clipper Ship, 1860
London to New York in 504 hours.

S.S. Oceanic, 1910
London to New York in 280 hours.

DC-4, 1960
London to New York in 12 hours.

Concorde, 1985
London to New York in 3½ hours.

Travel makes the globe seem smaller. What effects do inventions like the telephone, radio, and satellite television have on the globe?

A Twenty-four Hour Clock

This page shows what time it is, and what's happening at one particular moment all around the world. For instance, people in Montreal, Canada are eating breakfast while people in London, England are eating lunch.

If it is 7:00 a.m. in Montreal, what time is it where you live? Compare what you do at this time of the day to what people are doing around the world.

If it takes seven hours to fly from London to Montreal, and your flight leaves at 12:00 p.m., what time will it be in Montreal when you get there?

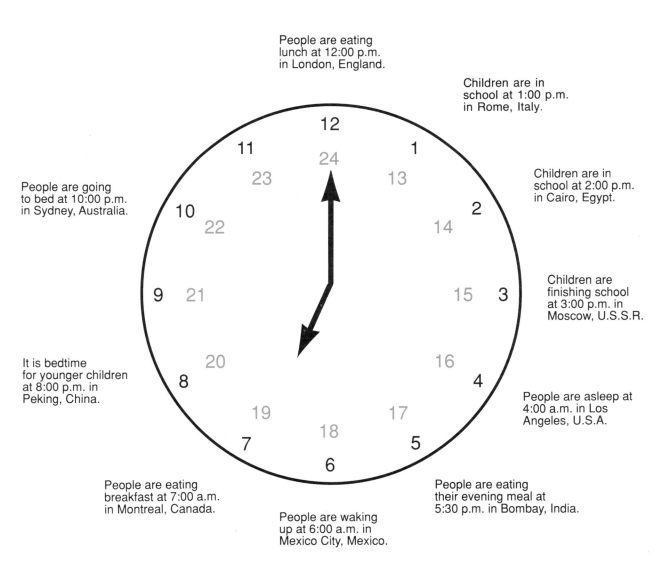

People are eating lunch at 12:00 p.m. in London, England.

Children are in school at 1:00 p.m. in Rome, Italy.

Children are in school at 2:00 p.m. in Cairo, Egypt.

People are going to bed at 10:00 p.m. in Sydney, Australia.

Children are finishing school at 3:00 p.m. in Moscow, U.S.S.R.

It is bedtime for younger children at 8:00 p.m. in Peking, China.

People are asleep at 4:00 a.m. in Los Angeles, U.S.A.

People are eating breakfast at 7:00 a.m. in Montreal, Canada.

People are waking up at 6:00 a.m. in Mexico City, Mexico.

People are eating their evening meal at 5:30 p.m. in Bombay, India.

Look up the location of each of these places in an atlas, or on a globe of the world.

Great Circle Routes

Transportation developments have made it possible to travel very quickly between different places in the world. It is now possible to travel from Vancouver to Stockholm in 8 hours 55 minutes, and from Toronto to Amsterdam in 6 hours 50 minutes. In the air or on the oceans, routes of travel are based on the globe and not on a flat map. It is easier to plot a route on a globe than on a map. The globe gives a more accurate picture of the earth.

If you want to find the shortest distance from Vancouver to Stockholm, stretch a piece of string between the two cities. What happens when the string is stretched beyond the two cities, going in what seems to be a straight line? These shortest routes are called Great Circle Routes. Any circle which cuts the globe into two equal parts is called a Great Circle Route.

The Earth from Space 1

If you were to travel into space, you could be far enough away to see the Earth as a globe. Over the North Pole you would see the Earth as it appears on this page. The part of the Earth you see is called the *Northern Hemisphere*. Notice that the North Pole is in water.

The Northern Hemisphere

1. Compare this map view with a globe. Can you see the equator when you look down at the globe?

2. Is there more land or more water in the Northern Hemisphere?

The Earth from Space 2

If you were in space over the South Pole you would see the Earth as it appears here. The part of the Earth you see is called the *Southern Hemisphere*.

The Southern Hemisphere

1. Compare this map view with a globe. Can you see the equator?

2. Is the South Pole in land or in water?

3. Is there more land or more water in the Southern Hemisphere?

Apollo Snapshot 1

This spectacular NASA photograph was taken from the Apollo 11 spacecraft during its voyage toward the moon. The Apollo 11, with astronauts Neil A. Armstrong, Michael Collins, and Edwin E. Aldrin, Jr. aboard, was already about 98,000 nautical miles (which is approximately 180 thousand kilometres) from Earth when this picture was taken.

NASA

1. What does NASA stand for?

2. Describe what features of the Earth you see in this photograph.

GLOBE

Apollo Snapshot 2

This NASA photograph
shows a view of North
America. Use a map or globe
of the Earth to identify the
features you can see.

NASA

Bearings Show Direction

A compass is one way of finding out direction. If a compass shows four points, the angles between the points are 90°. If the compass shows eight points, the angles are 45°. North-east is 45° from north. It can also be said that the *bearing* of north-east from north is 45°.

South-east is 135° from north. Its bearing is 135°. South-west is 225° from north. Its bearing is 225°. What is the bearing of west from north? Notice that bearings are always measured from north in a clockwise direction. The bearing for west is, therefore, 270°.

If there are four angles of 90° or eight angles of 45° in a compass rose, how many degrees would there be if you started at north and went all the way around to north?

Bearings are used at sea, in cross-country skiing, in orienteering and in flying. Bearings are used because they offer a common way to describe direction.

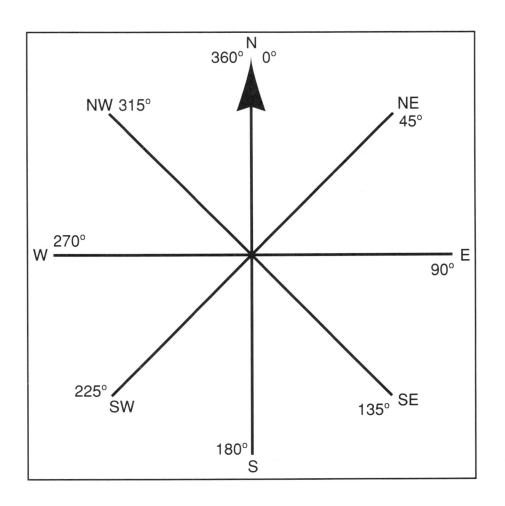

Air-Sea Rescue

It is possible to combine two bearings to show a particular location. When a bearing is taken, a line may be drawn on a map from the point where the bearing is taken in the direction of the bearing. Sometimes it is useful to pinpoint the exact location of an object. Two bearings on the same object are taken from two different locations. The point where the two lines cross is the location of the object.

Read the story that follows. Draw the map on page 83 in your notebook so you can carry out the rescue instructions.

Air-Sea Rescue

Imagine you are the commander of an air-sea rescue unit stationed at Halifax, Nova Scotia. It is late in February, a time of storms and drifting ice. You must always be alert for distress signals, and aware of the ice and weather conditions in your area.

You have a number of short-wave radio communication links to keep you up-to-date. The locations of these eight radio communication links are shown on the map on page 83. You also have an aircraft at Halifax and Gander, and patrol boats stationed at Halifax, Glace Bay, Port aux Basques, Marystown, and St. John's.

At two o'clock in the afternoon you receive a message that a fishing boat from Port aux Basques is adrift. You immediately instruct the short-wave radio operators in your area to be on the alert for further distress signals. You need to know the position of the boat at the various times so that you can find out its drift. The situation is complicated because a storm is brewing in the area. It may be some time before an aircraft can participate in the rescue attempt.

Rescue Instructions:
To start the rescue you must first locate the position of the fishing boat from its original distress message. At this time the boat had a bearing of 277° from Port aux Basques and 35° from Moncton. To find the fishing boat's location, plot each bearing and draw the necessary lines from each place to where they intersect. This is the position of the first distress call.

Plot each of the remaining three calls in the same way. Draw a dotted line to join the four plotted positions. This line gives the approximate direction of the drift of the fishing boat.

Rescue helicopters are sent from Gander as soon as the weather is clear. By the time the helicopters reach the fishing boat it has drifted a further 50 kilometres. What is the bearing of the fishing boat now from Gander?

You send a ship from St. John's to tow the fishing boat into port. By the time the ship reaches the fishing boat, it has drifted another 100 kilometres. What is the bearing of the fishing boat from St. John's?

Distress Call	From 2	From 3	From 5	From 6	From 7	From 8
A	277°				35°	
B				358°		60°
C		260°	55°			
D	140°		67°			

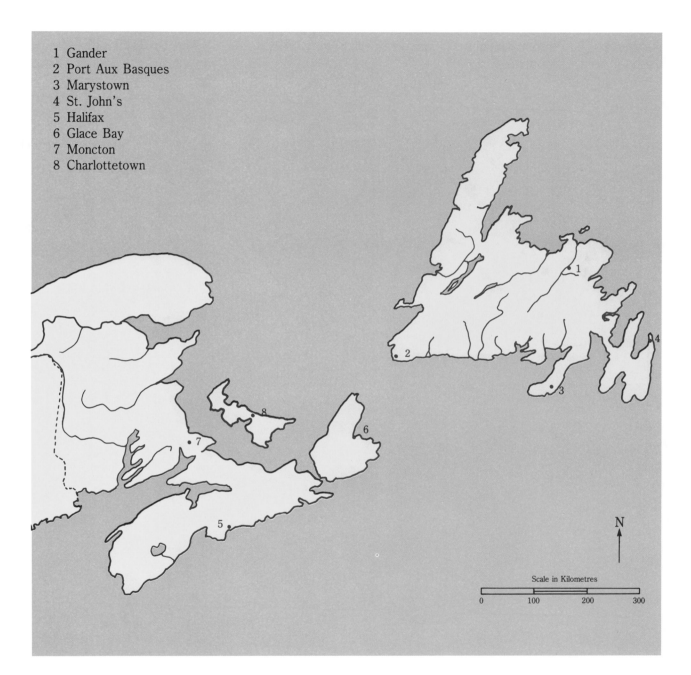

1 Gander
2 Port Aux Basques
3 Marystown
4 St. John's
5 Halifax
6 Glace Bay
7 Moncton
8 Charlottetown

Scale in Kilometres

0   100   200   300

N

Migratory Bird Routes

Birds and animals often travel very long distances, sometimes crossing international boundaries. They always manage to know which directions to travel in spite of barriers people may build.

This map shows three bird migration routes in the Western Hemisphere.

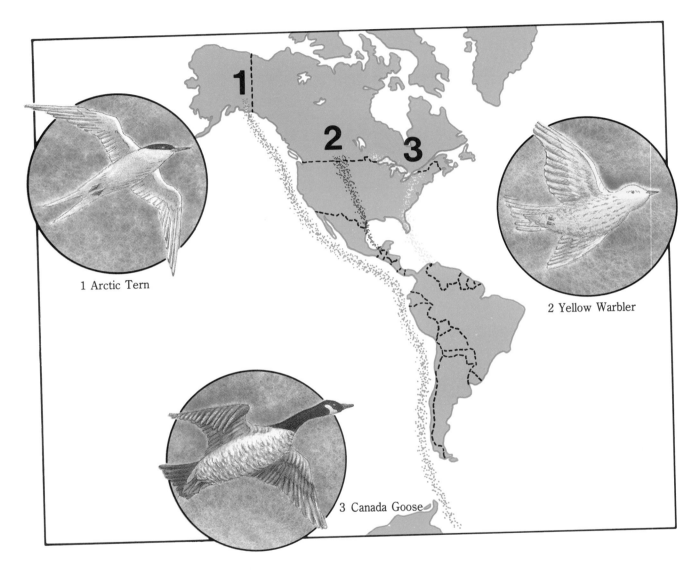

1 Arctic Tern

2 Yellow Warbler

3 Canada Goose

Find a map of the Western Hemisphere in an atlas. See if you can identify, as closely as possible, where the birds migrate from, and the places they migrate to. Record your observations on a chart like this.

Bird	Migrates from	Migrates to

Relief Symbols

Contour lines join places of equal height and show the relief of the land. Contour lines make it possible to show the shape of a hill. *Contour intervals* help to show how steep the hill is.

A contour interval is the space between two contour lines. In other words, the interval is the difference between the heights of two lines. The closer the contour lines, the steeper the relief.

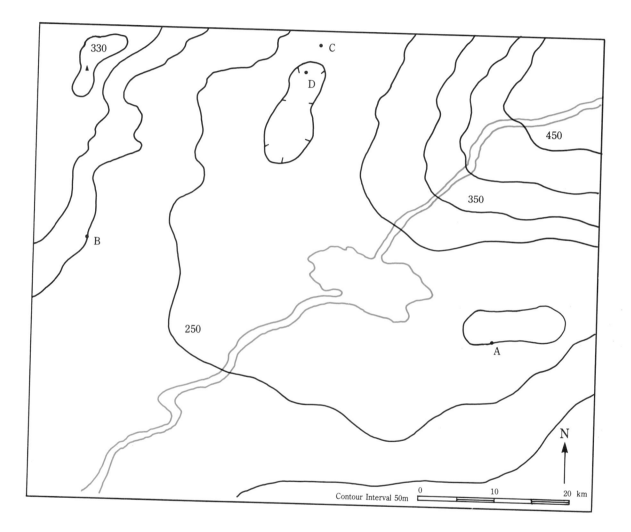

330

• C

D

450

350

B

250

A

N

Contour Interval 50m   0   10   20 km

1. In which general direction does the river flow? How do you know?

2. What are the heights of points A and B?

3. What does the number 330 mean on the map?

4. Is point D higher or lower than point C?

5. What is the approximate height of the lake?

6. Over which part of its course does the river flow faster, above the lake or below the lake?

Different Points of View

It is often useful to look at something from different points of view. If you are in a helicopter looking straight down at a hill, the shape you see can be drawn as a contour line diagram.

If you are standing on the ground looking at the hill, the shape looks different. This shape is called the profile. The following drawings show the same hill from these two points of view.

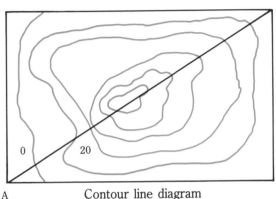

Contour line diagram

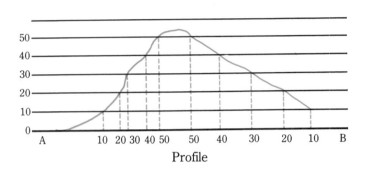

Profile

Sometimes it is useful to show a change in height without showing a complete hill. The following diagrams show how a change in height might be shown.

List examples of changes in relief in your community. Use some examples of obvious, even dramatic, changes in height of land. Think of other examples that show smaller or gradual changes in height.

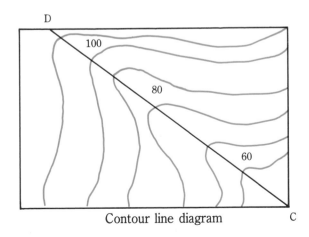

Contour line diagram

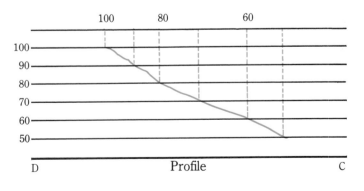

Profile

How Land Is Used 1

One of the most common symbols used on maps is colour. Colour is used to show many things. For example, colour can be used to show relief. Colour can also be used to show how land is used. In a city it might be useful to know where the land is used for industry or recreation. In rural areas it might be necessary to know which crops are grown.

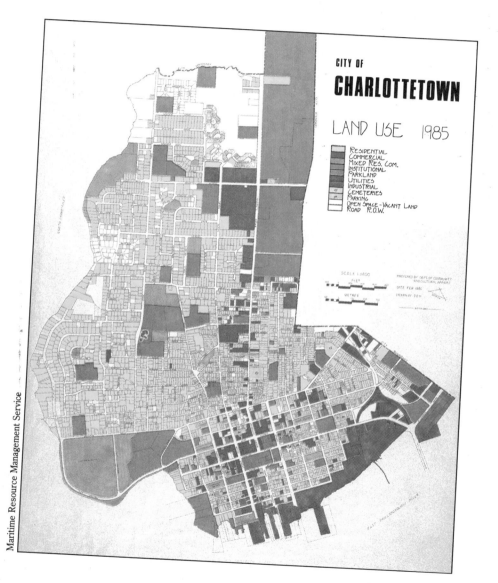

Maritime Resource Management Service

1. Refer to an atlas to list five ways maps use colour as a symbol.

2. What do the green areas on this map represent? Look at other maps, including a map of your community, to see how the colour green is used as a symbol.

SYMBOLS

How Land Is Used 2

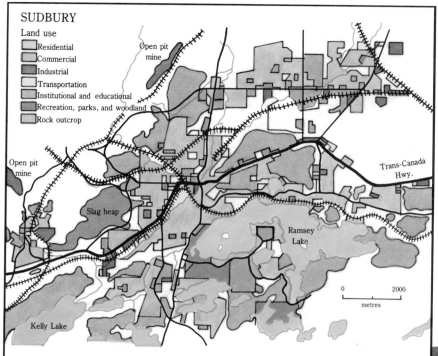

SUDBURY

Land use
- Residential
- Commercial
- Industrial
- Transportation
- Institutional and educational
- Recreation, parks, and woodland
- Rock outcrop

Open pit mine

Open pit mine

Slag heap

Kelly Lake

Ramsey Lake

Trans-Canada Hwy.

0   2000
metres

This is a land use map of Sudbury, Ontario. What does it show about land use in urban and nonurban areas?

This is an aerial photograph of Sudbury. What does it show about land use? Compare the photograph and the map of Sudbury?

Dionne Photography

SYMBOLS

Land Use Map of Winnipeg

This is a map of the city of Winnipeg. It shows the way land is used. Can you describe in terms of location which parts of the city are residential, commercial, industrial, parkland and institutional? Think of reasons for the location of each.

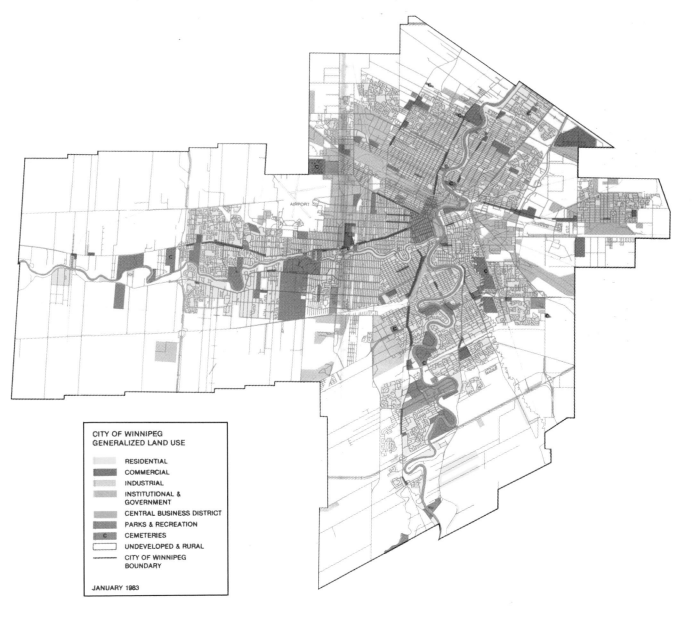

CITY OF WINNIPEG
GENERALIZED LAND USE

RESIDENTIAL
COMMERCIAL
INDUSTRIAL
INSTITUTIONAL &
GOVERNMENT
CENTRAL BUSINESS DISTRICT
PARKS & RECREATION
C   CEMETERIES
UNDEVELOPED & RURAL
CITY OF WINNIPEG
BOUNDARY

JANUARY 1983

AIRPORT

Drawing to Different Scales 1

Sketch maps are easiest to make if you use a photograph and draw a map the same size. This is not always possible. At times, it is necessary to sketch a smaller (scaled-down) version or a larger (scaled-up) version.

The sketch map on this page has been started using a larger scale than the photograph. Using graph paper, copy the section of the map which has been started. Complete the sketch map.

Canada's famous Hospital for Sick Children is located in Toronto. Can you find it in the photograph?

Photo courtesy Ontario Hydro

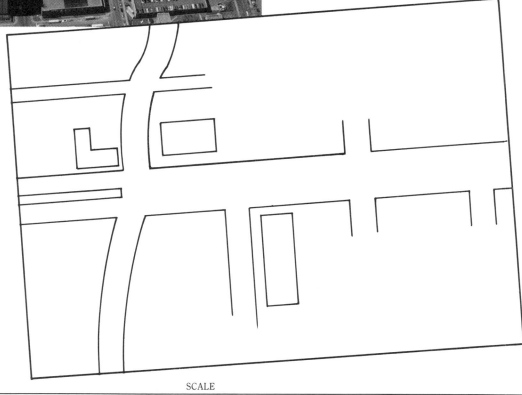

SCALE

Drawing to Different Scales 2

Use the photograph of Calgary, Alberta on this page to practise drawing sketch maps to both smaller and larger scales.

Jerry Davidson

Distances on a Map

A legend shows all the symbols used on a map. Similarly, a scale shows what distances stand for on a map. A map's scale compares the distance on a map to the real distance of a place on Earth.

Not all maps have the same scale. A centimetre might represent a large distance or a small distance on a map, depending on what detail needs to be shown.

When you understand how to use a map's scale, you can find real distances between places on Earth.

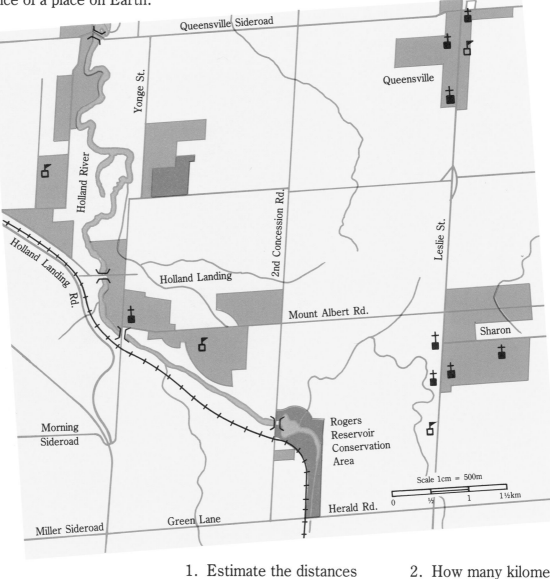

1. Estimate the distances between the four bridges on the Holland River.

2. How many kilometres is the Rogers Reservoir Conservation area from Sharon? from Queensville?

Important Parallels of Latitude

Latitude and longitude are imaginary lines used to locate places on the Earth. The equator is the base-line for measuring latitude. It divides the Earth into equal halves or hemispheres. All lines of latitude run parallel to the equator which is why they are called parallels of latitude. The equator and several other important lines of latitude are usually shown on a map or globe of the world.

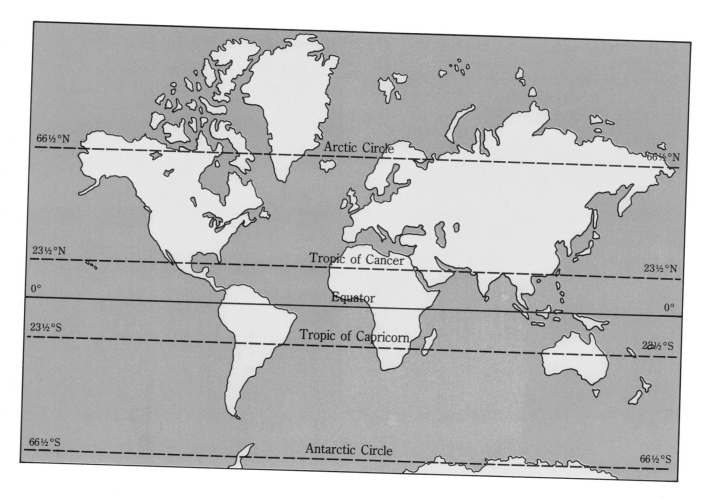

1. Locate these parallels of latitude on a globe of the world.

2. Which continents and oceans does each imaginary line of latitude pass through?

Grid Lines and Reference Numbers

The grid on a topographic map is useful for determining location. Find the blue grid lines and reference numbers on this topographic map of the Gander, Newfoundland region.

Find the arena in Gander. The following five steps show how to find a grid reference number for the arena to the nearest 100 metres.

1. Read the number on the grid line immediately to the left of the arena. The number is 74.

2. Estimate, in tenths of a square, how far east the arena is from this grid line. The estimated number is 3.

   Steps one and two are called *easting*. The easting reference number for the arena is 743.

3. Now, read the number on the grid line immediately below the arena. The number is 25.

4. Estimate, in tenths of a square, how far north the arena is from this grid line. The estimated number is 5.

   Steps three and four are called *northing*. The northing reference number for the arena is 255.

5. The grid reference number for the arena is given as 743255. Work backwards from this number to see if you can find the arena.

Locating a Community

There are usually reasons why a community is located in a certain place. Geographical factors which existed at the time a community was founded usually continue to affect the growing community.

Below are examples of four types of communities. Give possible reasons for each community's location.

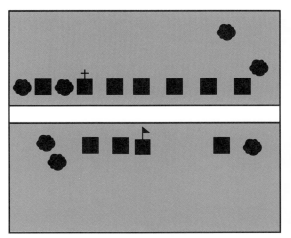

A community that follows a road or river, and is long and ribbonlike.

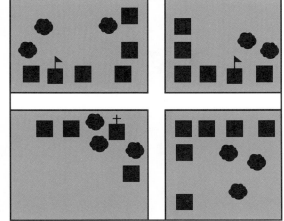

A community that is clustered around a road junction.

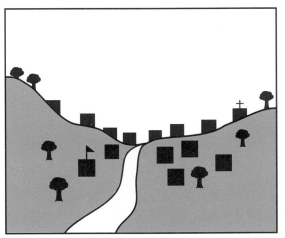

A community in a valley with fertile land.

A coastal community developed in a sheltered harbour.

1. Think of reasons for your own community's location.

2. Choose any community in Canada other than your own. Why do you think it is located where it is?

Settlement Patterns

As well as showing geographic information, maps and drawings can show information about people's settlement patterns.

The two maps on this page show information about historical settlement patterns in Nova Scotia. Where did the original groups settle? Why do you think they settled where they did?

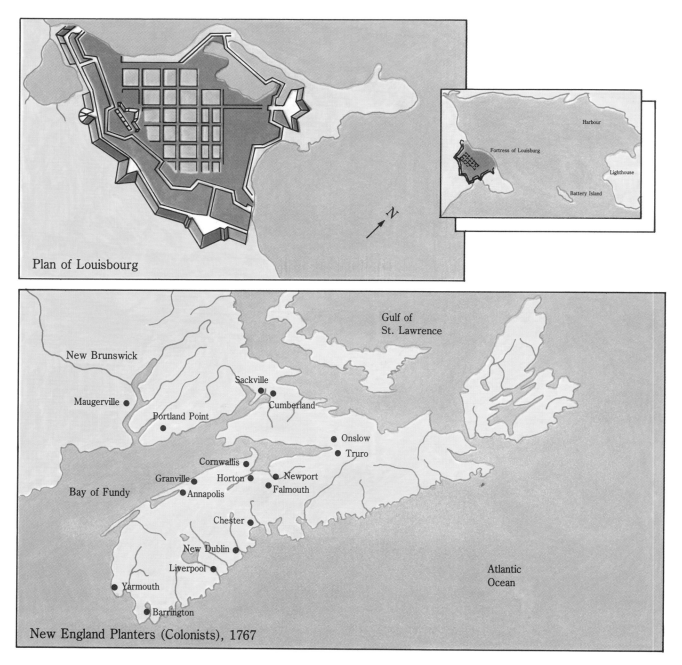

Plan of Louisbourg

Harbour

Fortress of Louisburg

Lighthouse

Battery Island

N

Gulf of St. Lawrence

New Brunswick

Maugerville

Sackville

Cumberland

Portland Point

Onslow

Truro

Cornwallis

Granville

Horton

Newport

Annapolis

Falmouth

Bay of Fundy

Chester

New Dublin

Liverpool

Yarmouth

Barrington

Atlantic Ocean

New England Planters (Colonists), 1767

Using Time Lines

The time lines on this page show periods of 100 years or more. Draw both time lines in your notebook, and complete the questions and instructions that accompany them.

1. Can you label the mark which stands for 1950?

2. Label the other marks.

3. Draw lines and label where 1925 and 1975 should be.

4. Mark the present year and label it.

A.
A time line can be made quite simply by drawing marks on a line. On this time line, a mark is shown for each decade, or ten-year period.

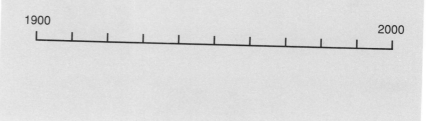

1900   2000

B.
Time lines are one way to show a sequence of historical events. Here is a partially completed time line showing some Canadian explorers. Add the explorers whose voyages are shown on the map on page 60.

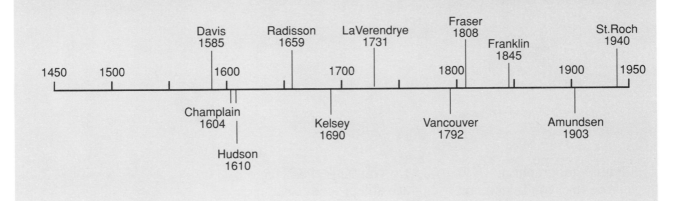

The Growth of a City

Winnipeg is an example of a community that continues to grow. The original factors that led to its location are still present. However, some of them may decrease in importance as other factors become more important.

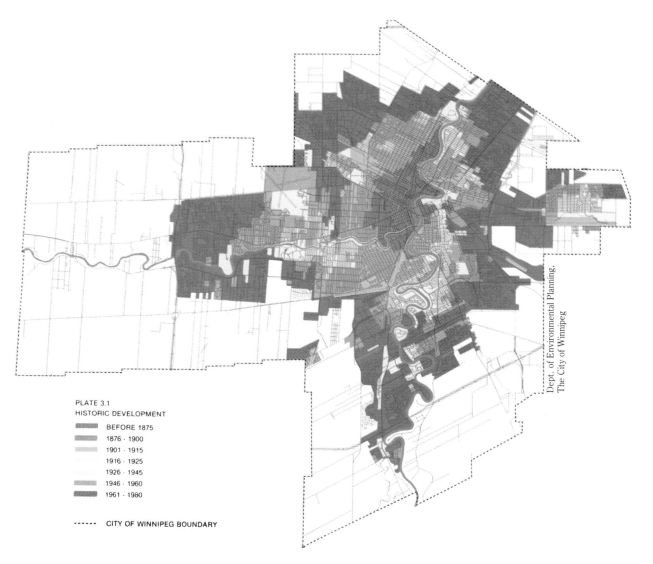

PLATE 3.1
HISTORIC DEVELOPMENT

▨ BEFORE 1875
▨ 1876 - 1900
▨ 1901 - 1915
  1916 - 1925
  1926 - 1945
▨ 1946 - 1960
▨ 1961 - 1980

------ CITY OF WINNIPEG BOUNDARY

Dept. of Environmental Planning,
The City of Winnipeg

1. Identify geographical factors that you think may have led to the location of Winnipeg.

2. Do you think these factors are still present today? Identify new factors that may play a part in the growth of the city.

Thematic Maps

A globe is a more accurate way to show the earth than a map. However, it is often necessary to use a map to show a particular kind of information. A *theme* gives information on one topic. A *thematic map* shows information on one topic.

An example of an important theme is interdependence. *Interdependence* means that people depend on the efforts of others for what they need. For example, Canadians depend on people in other places with warmer climates for fresh produce during the winter. People throughout the world are dependent on others for many of their needs.

The thematic map on this page shows the major trade routes and canals of the world today.

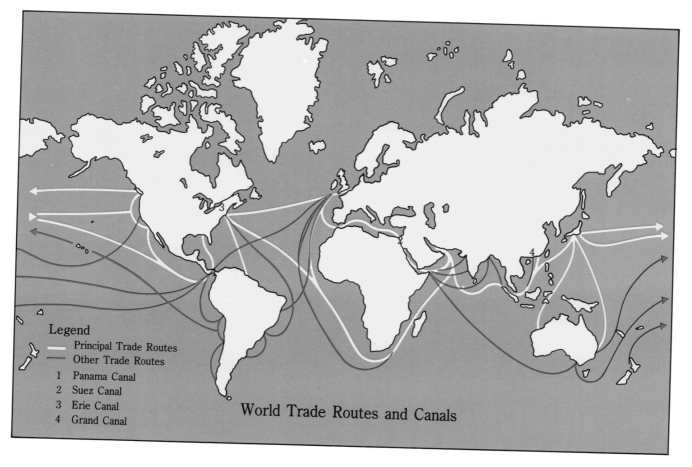

Legend
— Principal Trade Routes
— Other Trade Routes
1 Panama Canal
2 Suez Canal
3 Erie Canal
4 Grand Canal

World Trade Routes and Canals

1. Use this thematic map to describe, in words, the pattern of trade in the world.

2. Why do you think there is trading between countries?

3. What is a canal? How have canals affected world trade?

4. Use an atlas or a globe of the world to identify the major trading centres shown on this map.

North Is Not Always Up

Finding the direction of north on a map has a lot to do with location. If a map is on a wall, north is thought to be up or in the direction of the top of the map.

If a map is on the floor with the top of the map facing north, north is no longer up. It is more accurately the direction towards the North Pole.

If you stand at the North Pole, north is in a different direction altogether. The directions east and west also look different at the North Pole. East and west follow the direction of the parallels of latitude. From the North Pole these parallels look like circles.

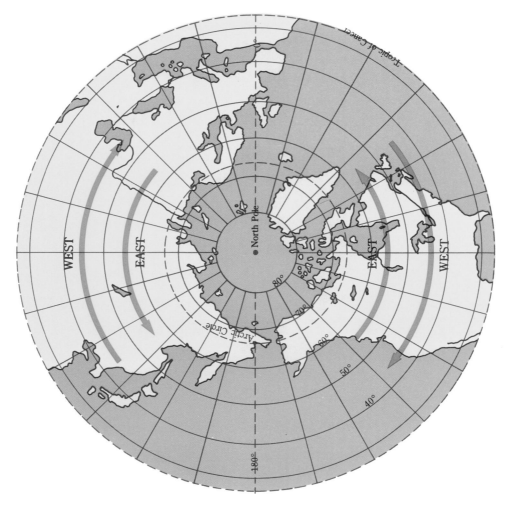

Notice the arrows that show the directions east and west. If you stand at the North Pole, which arm points east and which points west?

Symbols Show Quantities 1

It is often helpful to use symbols to show quantities. A symbol can be given a definite quantity, or a large symbol can simply show more than a small symbol.

This map uses a series of increasingly larger symbols to show the number of flights per year from Canada's international, national and regional airports. When symbols are used to show increasing amounts, they are called *graduated symbols*.

Airports
△ International
■ National
• Regional

80 000 --- 50 000
25 000 --- 10 000
5 000 ---

Number of Flights per Year

1. List Canada's international, national and regional airports.

2. Approximately how many flights per year are made from each airport?

3. What do the symbols tell you about air transportation in Canada?

Symbols Show Quantities 2

This map shows a different way to use graduated symbols.

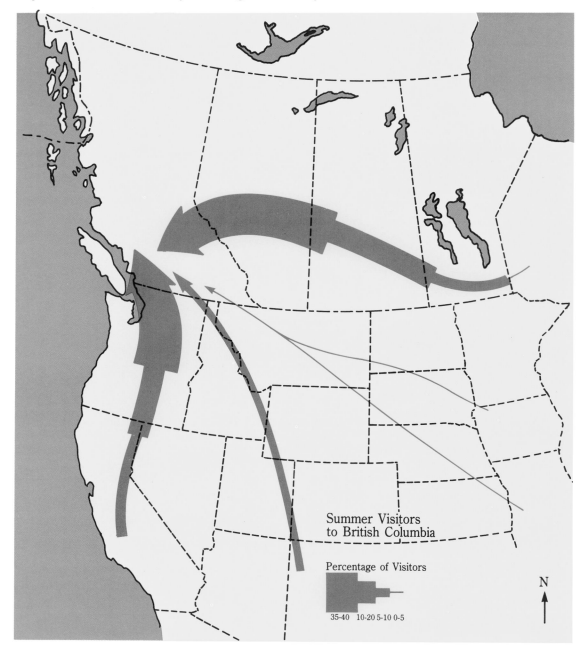

Summer Visitors
to British Columbia

Percentage of Visitors

35-40 10-20 5-10 0-5

N

1. What do the symbols tell you about the summer visitors to British Columbia?

2. What information is not provided by the symbols?

3. How is this map similar to the map on page 101? How is it different?

A Population Map

The population map of Canada on this page shows how many people live in Canada, and the provinces and territories in which they live. This map also shows something about the population density of Canada. *Population density* means how many people inhabit a specified area.

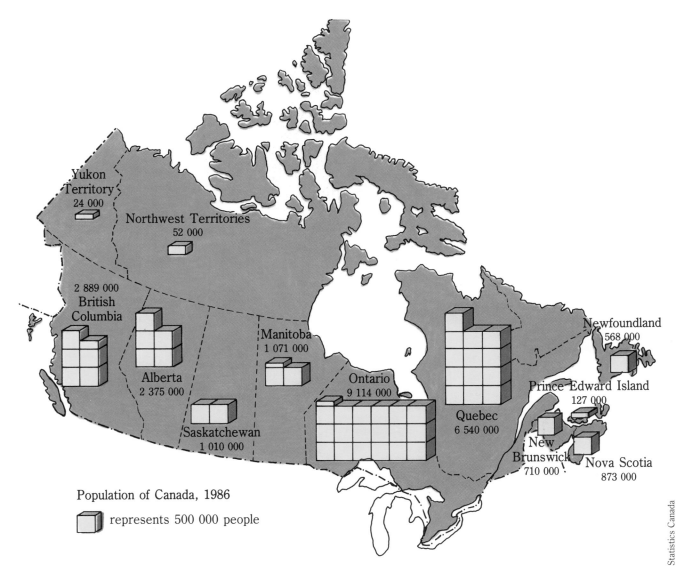

Yukon Territory 24 000

Northwest Territories 52 000

2 889 000 British Columbia

Alberta 2 375 000

Saskatchewan 1 010 000

Manitoba 1 071 000

Ontario 9 114 000

Quebec 6 540 000

Newfoundland 568 000

Prince Edward Island 127 000

New Brunswick 710 000

Nova Scotia 873 000

Population of Canada, 1986

represents 500 000 people

Statistics Canada

1. Which provinces and territories have the largest populations? Which have the smallest?

2. What does this map show about the distribution of Canada's population?

3. How do you think Canada's geography has affected settlement patterns?

Immigrants to Canada

Canada's immigrants come from places all around the world. The line graphs on this page show the number, and places of origin, of Canada's immigrants for the years 1982 to 1985.

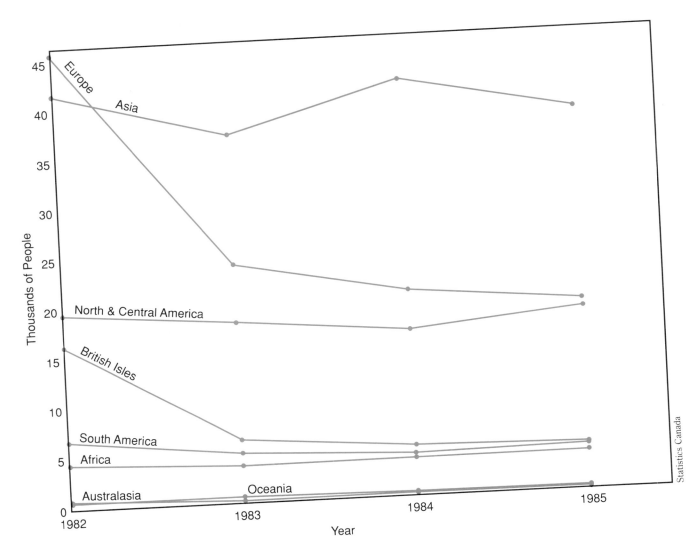

Thousands of People

Europe

Asia

North & Central America

British Isles

South America

Africa

Australasia

Oceania

Statistics Canada

1982   1983   1984   1985

Year

1. What areas of the world did most of Canada's immigrants come from?

2. What areas had the most consistent number of immigrants to Canada?

3. What areas have had large decreases in the number of immigrants to Canada?

4. What areas have had increases in the number of immigrants to Canada?

5. Name several countries that belong to each of these eight areas.

Exports and Imports

The two circle graphs on this page show the various goods which Canada imports and exports. The figures are for the year 1986.

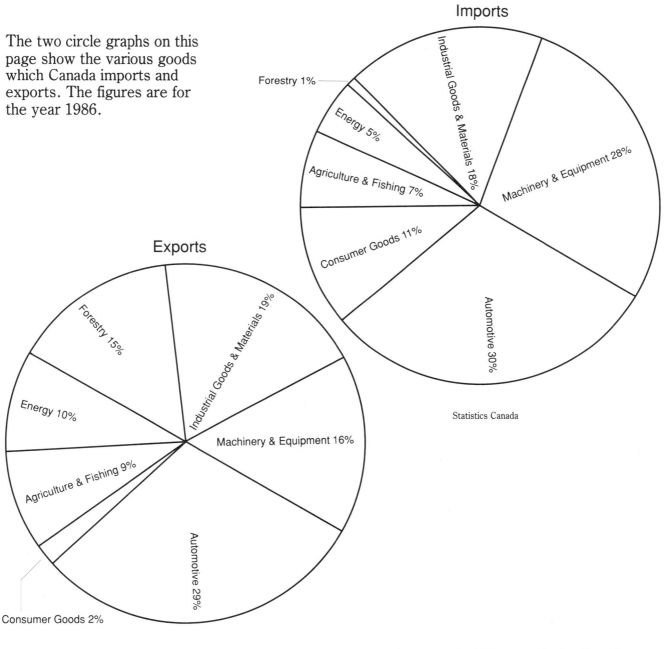

Imports

Forestry 1%

Industrial Goods & Materials 18%

Energy 5%

Machinery & Equipment 28%

Agriculture & Fishing 7%

Consumer Goods 11%

Automotive 30%

Statistics Canada

Exports

Foresty 15%

Industrial Goods & Materials 19%

Energy 10%

Machinery & Equipment 16%

Agriculture & Fishing 9%

Automotive 29%

Consumer Goods 2%

1. What are Canada's largest imports and exports?

2. What are Canada's smallest imports and exports?

3. What goods do Canadians import and export in comparable amounts?

4. What goods do Canadians import in a larger quantity than they export them?

Climate Graphs

A *climate graph* shows both temperature and precipitation. What two kinds of graphs have been used to make these climate graphs?

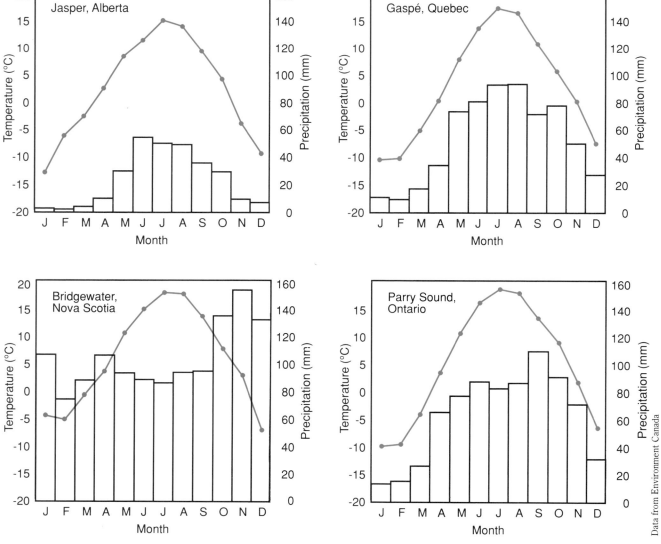

1. What can you say about each city's climate?

2. Find data on temperature and precipitation for your location and draw a climate graph.

Locating Places in North America

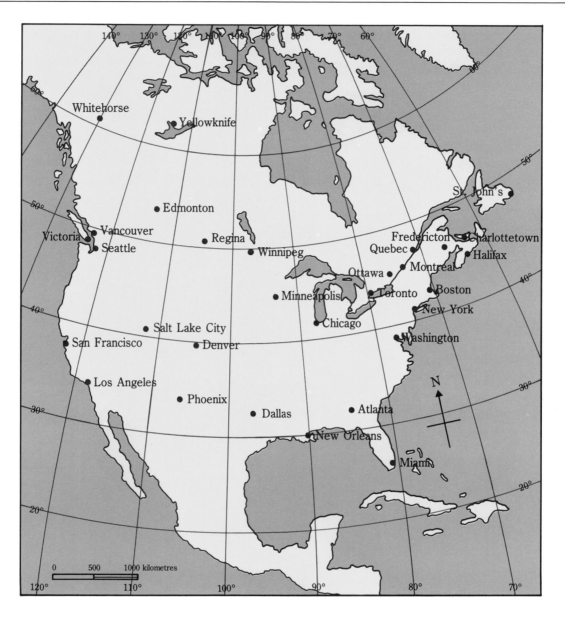

1. Give the location (latitude and longitude) for Victoria, Phoenix, Winnipeg, and Boston.

2. Identify the cities at these locations: 62°N 114°W, 41°N 87°W, 45°N 73°W, and 30°N 90°W.

3. Which city is farther west, Edmonton or Denver?

4. Which city is farther east, Ottawa or Washington?

5. Which city on the map is farthest north? south? east? west?

6. In which direction is the Prime Meridian from Canada? In which direction is the equator?

The Four Seasons

The Earth spins, or revolves around an imaginary line called its axis. The Earth's axis is tilted. The Earth's tilt and its orbit around the sun cause the change in seasons.

In the summer, the Northern Hemisphere tilts directly towards the sun. It receives the sun's direct rays. The days are longer and as a result the Northern Hemisphere gets more heat from the sun.

In the winter, the Northern Hemisphere tilts directly away from the sun. It receives the sun's indirect or slanted rays. The days are shorter, and the Northern Hemisphere gets less heat from the sun.

In the spring and fall, the Northern Hemisphere tilts neither directly towards nor away from the sun.

The Northern and Southern Hemispheres have opposite seasons.

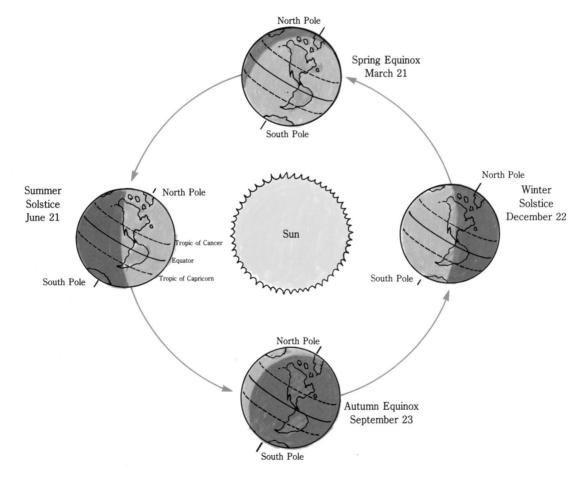

The sun illuminates half of the Earth while the other half is in darkness. On only two days of the year, the length of the day and the length of the night are exactly the same. What are these two days?

World Time

Time zones throughout the world are based on longitude. Time changes one hour for every 15 degrees of longitude. Each meridian of longitude falls in the centre of a time zone. Time zones vary a bit for the sake of convenience.

This map shows the time zones of the world. Each time zone is shown with a positive or negative number which indicates how its standard time differs from Greenwich Mean Time.

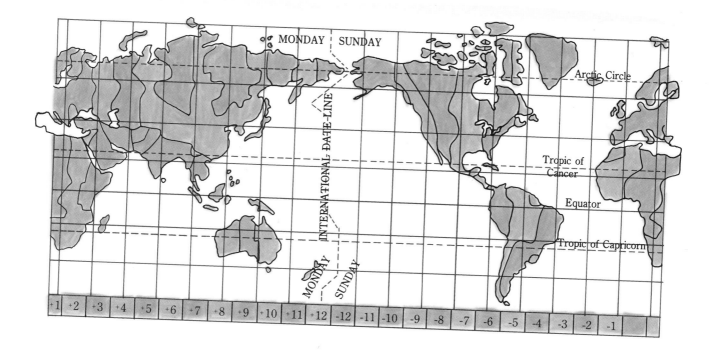

1. How many time zones is the surface of the Earth divided into?

2. What is the difference between your time and Greenwich Mean Time?

3. If time zones followed exactly the paths of the meridians, what sorts of problems could there be?

The International Date Line

Exactly opposite the Prime Meridian, is the International Date Line. Its latitude is 180°.

The International Date Line zig zags around land masses so the people who live in one country will not only have the same time, but they will also be on the same day.

Everyone calculates their time from the Prime Meridian. So, people travelling *eastward* from the Prime Meridian would be 12 hours ahead of Greenwich Time when they arrived at the International Date Line. But, people travelling *westward* from the Prime Meridian would be 12 hours behind Greenwich Time when they arrived at the International Date Line. There is a 24-hour difference in these two times. To correct the situation, people must add or subtract a day, depending on the direction they are travelling, at the International Date Line.

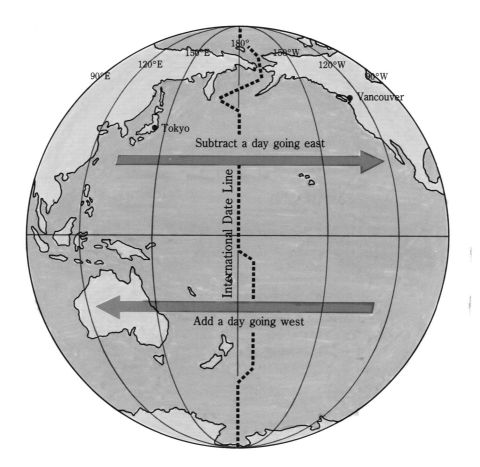

1. If you left Vancouver on Monday and travelled westward to Tokyo, what day is it when you arrive?

2. If you left Tokyo on Thursday and travelled eastward to Vancouver, what day is it when you arrive?

New World Technology

Modern advances in technology make many things possible. For instance, the following photograph of the James Bay Power Project shows how people can use technology to create landscape.

Look at a map of Canada to find James Bay. You will see that James Bay is an extension of Hudson Bay. The James Bay territory is part of the geographical region called the Canadian Shield. James Bay is bordered by Quebec and Ontario.

The James Bay Power Project is one of the largest hydroelectric projects in the world. It has doubled Quebec's hydro power and employed many people. The project has also been concerned with the protection of wildlife and the environment.

Spring runoff at the La Grande 2 spillway.

Hydro-Québec

1. What do you see in this photograph?

2. How have people changed the environment of the area?

3. How might a project like this affect wildlife and the environment?

4. For a class report, find examples of other projects in Canada and the world where there have been large-scale changes in the landscape.

Landsat Images

Modern technology makes it possible to show information in many ways. Page 111 shows a photograph of the James Bay Power Project. This page shows James Bay in a different way.

Satellites in space can take a picture that does not look like a picture taken with a camera. Most satellite pictures come from Landsat satellites that the United States has been launching since 1972. A Landsat satellite orbits the Earth and scans a strip of the Earth's surface 185 kilometres wide. The satellite orbits the Earth fourteen times a day. Every sixteen days it passes over the same spot on the Earth's surface.

To take pictures, a large mirror captures light from the Earth's surface. The light is coded into numbers on the satellite. These numbers are transmitted to a computer on the Earth which changes the numbers back to light patterns and adds colour. To understand a Landsat image, you have to learn to read the colours.

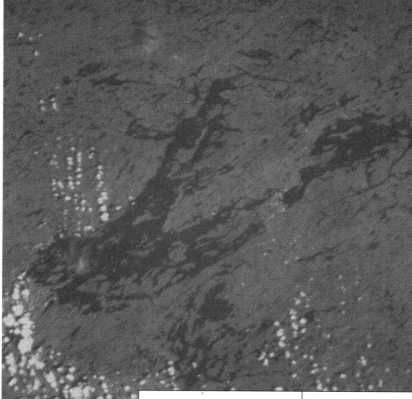

A Landsat image of La Grande 2 dam and spillway region of the James Bay Power Project.

LANDSAT imagery courtesy of the Canada Centre for Remote Sensing; Energy, Mines and Resources Canada.

red	growing vegetation: crops, grasslands, forests
pale pink to light brown	harvested cropland
white to very light brown	land with no vegetation, dry land with little moisture
browns and yellows	rocky land, range land
white	snow, ice, dense clouds
grey-blue	settled areas: cities, towns
light blue	shallow water, water clouded by silt, pollution
dark blue — blue black	deep or clear water
white in regular pattern	highways

Concepts

aerial photograph: a picture of the Earth taken from an aircraft.

Antarctic Circle: the imaginary line of latitude 66½° south of the equator.

Arctic Circle: the imaginary line of latitude 66½° north of the equator.

astronomy: a science that studies the planets and stars.

atlas: a book of maps.

autumn equinox: see *equinox*. The time of the year when the length of the day and the length of the night are the same; September 23.

axis: an imaginary straight line joining the north and south poles around which the earth spins or revolves.

bar graph: see *graph*. A bar graph uses boxes or rectangles to compare quantities.

bearing: a direction or position of an object in relation to something else.

block: 1. a space in a city or town bordered by four streets; 2. the length of one side of such a block; the buildings between two intersections.

border: a line that divides one place from another; a boundary.

canal: an artificial waterway.

capital: the city or town where the government of a country or province is located.

cardinal points: the four main directions of a compass; north, south, east and west.

cartographer: a person skilled in making maps and charts.

cartography: the making of maps and charts.

census: an official count of all the people in a country.

chart: any kind of diagram or table that gives information in an organized way.

circle graph: see *graph*. A circle graph uses a circle to show fractions or parts of a whole.

climate: the average weather conditions of an area over a long period of time.

colour: used as a symbol on maps, charts and graphs to show information.

compass: an instrument for telling direction. A magnetic needle turns freely on a pivot and points to the North Magnetic Pole.

compass rose: a symbol that shows eight direction points. The long points show the four cardinal directions.

continent: one of the seven large bodies of land on Earth. The seven continents are Africa, Asia, Australia, Europe, North America, South America and Antarctica.

contour line: a line on a map joining points of equal height.

contour map: a map showing different heights of the land using contour lines.

daylight-saving time: one hour ahead of standard time, giving more daylight in the evening.

direction: the point toward which something moves or faces; the relationship of one place to another.

east: the direction in which the sun rises; the direction to the right when facing north.

Eastern Hemisphere: see *hemisphere*. The half of the Earth east of the Atlantic Ocean, including Africa, Europe and Asia.

equator: an imaginary circle halfway between the North and South Poles that divides the Earth into two equal halves.

equinox: the two days in the year when the length of the day and the length of the night are the same. See *autumn equinox* and *spring equinox*.

exports: goods sent out of a country.

globe: a model of the Earth.

graduated symbols: the use of symbols to show increasing amounts.

graph: a line or diagram showing information. See *bar graph, circle graph, line graph, pictograph*.

Greenwich Mean Time: the time at Greenwich, England which is used internationally as a standard reference.

grid: a pattern of squares on a map.

grid map: a map with a grid drawn on it.

Great Circle Route: any circle that cuts the globe into two equal parts; the shortest distance between two points on the Earth's surface.

growing season: the length of time for growing and harvesting crops in which the weather is frost-free.

hemisphere: half of the Earth or globe.

imports: goods brought into a country.

interdependence: the reliance of people or events on each other.

International Date Line: an imaginary line in the Pacific Ocean where the date changes by one day when it is crossed; runs mostly along the 180° meridian of longitude.

landmark: a natural or artificial object that stands out in the landscape; used as a guide.

latitude: the distance north or south of the equator, measured in degrees.

legend: a list of the symbols used on a map.

line graph: see *graph*. A line graph uses a line to show an increase or decrease.

location: a position or place.

longitude: the distance east or west of the Prime Meridian, measured in degrees.

map: a drawing that represents part or all of the Earth's surface.

mapmaker: see *cartographer*.

meridians: imaginary lines joining the North and South Poles; lines of longitude.

month: one of the 12 parts of the year; lunar month: the time it takes the moon to orbit the Earth.

north: the direction towards the North Pole.

north indicator: the direction symbol on a map.

Northern Hemisphere: see *hemisphere*. The north half of the Earth or globe; the half of the globe north of the equator.

North Pole: the northernmost point on the Earth.

orbit: the path around the sun or any body in space.

orientation: finding direction or position in relation to one's surroundings; can involve using a compass.

orienteering: a sport in which people are given distance and direction clues to travel between points on a set course.

parallels: the imaginary lines that run parallel to the equator; lines of latitude.

photograph: a picture taken with a camera.

pictograph: see *graph*. A graph which uses a picture as a symbol.

pictorial symbol: a symbol that resembles what it represents.

population density: the number of people who live in a specified area.

precipitation: rain, snow, hail, sleet or fog.

Prime Meridian: the first line of longitude through Greenwich, England; 0° longitude.

profile: the side view of something.

relief: a word that describes the height of the land.

relief map: a map that shows the height of the land.

revolution: the movement of the Earth around the sun.

rotation: the turning of the Earth on its axis.

satellite: 1. an artificial object put into orbit around the Earth, moon, or a planet; 2. the natural moons of planets.

scale: a mathematical key to explain how far one place is from another on a map; helps show the size of an area.

sketch map: a drawing to show the important parts of a landscape.

south: the direction towards the South Pole.

Southern Hemisphere: see *hemisphere*. The south half of the Earth or globe; the half of the globe south of the equator.

South Pole: the southernmost point on the Earth.

spring equinox: see *equinox*. The time of the year when the length of the day and the length of the night are the same; March 21.

standard time: a country or area's official time based on Greenwich Mean Time.

symbol: something that stands for a real object.

thematic map: a map that shows information about one topic.

time: the passing hours, days, weeks, months and years.

time line: a graph that shows important events in the order in which they happened.

time zone: an area where a common standard time is used. The world is divided into 24 time zones.

topographic map: a map that shows the features of the Earth's surface.

Tropic of Cancer: the imaginary line of latitude 23½° north of the equator.

Tropic of Capricorn: the imaginary line of latitude 23½° south of the equator.

Universal Coordinated Time: see *Greenwich Mean Time*.

west: the direction in which the sun sets; the direction to the left when facing north.

Western Hemisphere: see *hemisphere*. The half of the Earth west of the Atlantic Ocean, including North and South America.

wheel graph: see *graph* and *circle graph*.

year: the time it takes the Earth to orbit the sun; 365 days (366 in a leap year).

Gazetteer

Annapolis Royal, N.S.	45°N	66°W	Gander, Nfld.	49°N	55°W	Miami, U.S.A.	39°N	85°W
Atlanta, U.S.A.	34°N	84°W	Gaspé, Quebec	49°N	64°W	Minneapolis, U.S.A.	45°N	93°W
			Glace Bay, N.S.	46°N	60°W			
			Goose Bay, Nfld.	53°N	60°W	Mississauga, Ontario	44°N	80°W
Bagotville, Quebec	48°N	71°W	Grande Prairie, Alberta	55°N	119°W	Moncton, N.B.	46°N	65°W
Baker Lake, N.W.T.	64°N	96°W	Grand Manan			Mont-Joli, Quebec	48°N	68°W
Banff, Alberta	51°N	116°W	Island, N.B.	45°N	67°W	Montreal, Quebec	46°N	74°W
Barrington, N.S.	43°N	66°W	Grimsby, Ontario	43°N	80°W	Moscow, U.S.S.R.	56°N	37°E
Bergen, Norway	51°N	4°E	Guelph, Ontario	43°N	80°W			
Berlin, Germany	52°N	13°E				Nairobi, Kenya	2°S	37°E
Bombay, India	19°N	73°E	Haines Junction,			New Orleans, U.S.A.	30°N	90°W
Boston, U.S.A.	42°N	71°W	Y.T.	61°N	137°W	Newport, N.S.	45°N	64°W
Brampton, Ontario	44°N	80°W	Halifax, N.S.	45°N	64°W	New York City, U.S.A.	41°N	74°W
Brandon, Manitoba	50°N	100°W	Hamilton, Ontario	43°N	80°W			
Brantford, Ontario	43°N	80°W	Holland Landing, Ontario	44°N	79°W	Niagara Falls, Ontario	43°N	79°W
Bridgewater, N.S.	44°N	64°W	Hull, Quebec	45°N	75°W	North Battleford, Saskatchewan	53°N	108°W
Burlington, Ontario	43°N	80°W				North Bay, Ontario	46°N	79°W
Cairo, Egypt	30°N	31°E	Jakarta, Indonesia	6°S	107°E			
Calcutta, India	22°N	88°E	Jasper, Alberta	53°N	118°W	Oakville, Ontario	43°N	80°W
Calgary, Alberta	51°N	114°W				Okanagan Falls, B.C.	50°N	120°W
Camrose, Alberta	53°N	113°W	Kamloops, B.C.	51°N	120°W	Oshawa, Ontario	44°N	79°W
Capetown, S. Africa	34°S	18°E	Kano, Nigeria	12°N	8°E	Ottawa, Ontario	45°N	75°W
Carcross, Y.T.	60°N	135°W	Karachi, Pakistan	25°N	67°E			
Charlottetown, P.E.I.	46°N	63°W	Kelowna, B.C.	50°N	119°W	Parry Sound, Ontario	45°N	80°W
Chatham, Ontario	42°N	82°W	Kingston, Ontario	44°N	76°W	Peking, China	40°N	116°E
Chester, N.S.	45°N	64°W	Kitchener, Ontario	43°N	80°W	Pelly Crossing, Y.T.	69°N	90°W
Chicago, U.S.A.	58°N	136°W				Penticton, B.C.	49°N	120°W
Cranbrook, B.C.	49°N	116°W	Leningrad, U.S.S.R.	60°N	30°E	Perth, Australia	32°S	116°E
			Lethbridge, Alberta	50°N	113°W	Peterborough, Ontario	44°N	78°W
Dakar, Senegal	15°N	17°W	Lisbon, Portugal	39°N	9°W	Phoenix, U.S.A.	34°N	112°W
Dallas, U.S.A.	33°N	97°W	Liverpool, N.S.	44°N	65°W	Prince George, B.C.	54°N	123°W
Dawson Creek, B.C.	56°N	120°W	Lloydminster, Alberta	53°N	110°W			
Deer Lake, Nfld.	49°N	58°W	London, England	51°N	0°W	Prince Rupert, B.C.	54°N	130°W
Denver, U.S.A.	40°N	105°W	Los Angeles, U.S.A.	34°N	118°W			
Dryden, Ontario	50°N	93°W	Louisbourg, N.S.	46°N	60°W	Quebec City, Quebec	47°N	71°W
Dundas, Ontario	43°N	80°W						
			Madras, India	13°N	80°E	Red Deer, Alberta	52°N	114°W
Edmonton, Alberta	54°N	114°W	Manila, Philippines	15°N	121°E			
			Marystown, Nfld.	47°N	55°W	Regina, Saskatchewan	50°N	104°W
Faro, N.W.T.	63°N	133°W	Mayo, Y.T.	63°N	136°W	Rome, Italy	42°N	12°E
Fort McMurray, Alberta	57°N	111°W	Medicine Hat, Alberta	50°N	111°W	Ross, Y.T.	62°N	132°W
Fort Nelson, B.C.	59°N	123°W	Mexico City, Mexico	19°N	99°W			
Fort St. John, B.C.	56°N	121°W						
Fredericton, N.B.	46°N	67°W						

Sackville, N.B.	46°N	64°W	Sharon, Ontario	44°N	79°W	Val-d'Or, Quebec	48°N	78°W
St. Catharines,			Simcoe, Ontario	43°N	80°W	Vancouver, B.C.	49°N	123°W
Ontario	43°N	79°W	Stephenville, Nfld.	49°N	69°W	Victoria, B.C.	48°N	123°W
Saint John, N.B.	45°N	66°W	Stockholm,					
St. John's, Nfld.	47°N	53°W	Sweden	59°N	18°E	Washington D.C.,		
Salt Lake City,			Sudbury, Ontario	46°N	81°W	U.S.A.	39°N	77°W
U.S.A.	41°N	112°W	Sydney, Australia	34°S	151°E	Waterloo, Ontario	43°N	81°W
San Francisco,			Sydney, N.S.	46°N	60°W	Whitehorse, Y.T.	60°N	135°W
U.S.A.	37°N	122°W				Windsor, Ontario	42°N	83°W
Sarnia, Ontario	43°N	82°W	Tashkent,			Winnipeg,		
Saskatoon,			U.S.S.R.	41°N	69°E	Manitoba	50°N	97°W
Saskatchewan	52°N	107°W	Teslin, Y.T.	60°N	132°W			
Saulte Ste. Marie,			Thunder Bay,			Yarmouth, N.S.	44°N	66°W
Ontario	46°N	84°W	Ontario	48°N	89°W	Yellowknife,		
Seattle, U.S.A.	47°N	122°W	Tokyo, Japan	36°N	140°E	N.W.T.	62°N	114°W
Sept-Îles, Quebec	50°N	66°W	Toronto, Ontario	44°N	79°W			
Shanghai, China	31°N	121°E	Truro, N.S.	45°N	63°W			